Human Rights

The Amherst Series in Law, Jurisprudence, and Social Thought

Each work included in The Amherst Series in Law, Jurisprudence, and Social Thought explores a theme crucial to an understanding of law as it confronts the changing social and intellectual currents of the twenty-first century.

Human Rights

Concepts, Contests, Contingencies

Edited by
AUSTIN SARAT
and
THOMAS R. KEARNS

Ann Arbor
THE UNIVERSITY OF MICHIGAN PRESS

Copyright © by the University of Michigan 2001
All rights reserved
Published in the United States of America by
The University of Michigan Press
Manufactured in the United States of America
⊗ Printed on acid-free paper

2004   2003   2002   2001   4   3   2   1

A CIP catalog record for this book is available from the British Library.

Library of Congress Cataloging-in-Publication Data

Human rights : concepts, contests, contingencies / edited by Austin
   Sarat and Thomas R. Kearns.
      p.   cm. — (The Amherst series in law, jurisprudence, and
   social thought)
   Includes index.
   ISBN 0-472-11192-2 (cloth : acid-free paper)
   1. Human rights.   2. Civil rights.   I. Sarat, Austin.   II. Kearns,
   Thomas R.   III. Series.
   JC571 .H765   2001
   323—dc21   00-010837

The lines from "Two: movement" from "Inscriptions," in *Dark Fields of the Republic: Poems, 1991–1995,* by Adrienne Rich, copyright © 1995 by Adrienne Rich. Used by permission of the author and W. W. Norton & Company, Inc.

Acknowledgments

We are grateful to our colleague Nasser Hussain for his help in shaping the ideas that inform this book. We thank our students in Amherst College's Department of Law, Jurisprudence, and Social Thought for their interest in the issues addressed in *Human Rights: Concepts, Contests, Contingencies.* Finally, we would like to express special appreciation for the generous financial support provided by Amherst College's Charles Hamilton Houston Forum on Law and Social Change and the Corliss Lamont Lectureship for a Peaceful World.

Contents

The Unsettled Status of Human Rights: An Introduction

Austin Sarat and Thomas R. Kearns

We respect the religious, social, and cultural characteristics that make each country unique. But we cannot let cultural relativism become the last refuge of repression.

Warren Christopher, address to the
World Conference on Human Rights, 1993

The concept of human rights, based upon the assumed existence of a human being as such, broke down at the very moment when those who professed to believe in it were for the first time confronted with the people who had indeed lost all other qualities and specific relationships—except that they were still human. The world found nothing sacred in the abstract nakedness of being human.

Hannah Arendt, *The Origins of Totalitarianism*

Fraternity is an inclination of the heart, one that produces a sense of shame at having much when others have little. It is not the sort of thing that anyone can have a theory about or that people can be argued into having.

Richard Rorty,
"Human Rights, Rationality, and Sentimentality"

"I believe and the American people believe," former President Clinton declared during a visit to the People's Republic of China, "that freedom of speech, association and religion are, as recognized by the United Nations Charter, the right of people everywhere and should be protected by their governments."[1] The next day, speaking to another audience in China, Clinton repeated his embrace of human rights. "We are convinced that certain rights are universal," he said. "I believe that everywhere people aspire to be treated with dignity, to give voice to their opinions, to choose their own leaders, to associate with whom they wish, to worship how, when, and where they want. These are not American rights or European rights or developed-world rights. They are the birthrights of people everywhere."[2] These statements, coming from an American president, were hardly surprising. While some might worry about the legitimacy or wisdom of a Western leader preaching human rights in a non-Western nation,[3] Clinton's statements exemplify the hegemonic, and yet fragile, hold of human rights on the political imagination of people in many parts of the world at the turn of the century.

Today the *language* of human rights, if not human rights themselves, is nearly universal.[4] Governments everywhere, including the government of the People's Republic of China,[5] claim to believe in and respect the dignity of their citizens,[6] even if they do not endorse the

---

1. *New York Times*, June 28, 1998, 9.

2. *Boston Globe*, June 29, 1998, A14.

3. See, for example, Adamantia Pollis and Peter Schwab, "Human Rights: A Western Construct with Limited Applicability," in *Human Rights: Cultural and Ideological Perspectives*, ed. Adamantia Pollis and Peter Schwab (New York: Praeger, 1979). As Sally Merry puts it, "Human rights is obviously based on Western liberal-legalist ideas, but in the postcolonial world, it is no longer exclusively owned by the West." "Legal Pluralism and Transnational Culture: The *Ka Ho'okolokolonui Kanaka Maoli* Tribunal, Hawaii, 1993," in *Human Rights, Culture, and Context: Anthropological Perspectives*, ed. Richard Wilson (London: Pluto Press, 1996), 29. For a useful general discussion of the question of whether human rights are Western see R. Pannikar, "Is the Notion of Human Rights a Western Concept?" *Diogenes* 120 (1982): 75.

4. "International human rights," David Weissbrodt claims, "is the world's first universal ideology." See "Human Rights: An Historical Perspective," in *Human Rights*, ed. P. Davies (London: Routledge, 1988). For a different perspective see Rhoda Howard, "Dignity, Community, and Human Rights," in *Human Rights in Cross-Cultural Perspectives: A Quest for Consensus*, ed. Abdullahi A. An-Na'im (Philadelphia: University of Pennsylvania Press, 1992). Howard argues that "most known human societies did not and do not have conceptions of human rights" (80).

5. See William Alford, "Making a Goddess of Democracy from Loose Sand: Thoughts on Human Rights in the People's Republic of China," in An-Na'im, *Human Rights*.

6. "We are witnessing an unequivocal process of universalization of the concern for human dignity." Fernando Teson, "International Human Rights and Cultural Relativism," *Virginia Journal of International Law* 25 (1985): 869. "[P]eople the world over," Parekh argues, "have frequently appealed to these principles in their struggles against

brand of human rights to which President Clinton would have them adhere.[7] This is not to say that everyone agrees on the meaning of human rights or what they entail.[8] This is surely not the case.[9] As the foreign minister of Singapore put it in a statement at the Vienna Conference on Human Rights, "[T]he extent and exercise of rights . . . varies greatly from one culture or political community to another . . . because [rights] are the products of the historical experiences of particular peoples."[10] Disagreements frequently arise over particular rights claims or the distinctive points of emphasis that shape the way a particular culture interprets the content of rights.[11] Moreover, even where there is agreement in principle, human rights are not universally respected in practice. However defined, they are variably realized; indeed they are

---

repressive governments. For their part the latter have almost invariably preferred to deny the existence of unacceptable practices rather than seek shelter behind relativism and cultural autonomy. In their own different ways both parties are thus beginning to accept the principles as the basis of good government, conferring on them the moral authority they otherwise cannot have." See Bhiku Parekh, "The Cultural Particularity of Liberal Democracy," in *Prospects for Democracy,* ed. David Held (Stanford, Calif.: Stanford University Press, 1993), 174. Donnelly contends that while concern for human dignity is central to non-Western cultural traditions, human rights are quite foreign to them. See Jack Donnelly, "Human Rights and Human Dignity: An Analytic Critique of Non-Western Conceptions of Human Rights," *American Political Science Review* 76 (1982): 303. See also Bilhari Kausikan, "Asia's Different Standard," *Foreign Policy* 92 (1993): 24.

7. While the leaders of Asian nations in the so called Bangkok Declaration (March 29, 1993) criticized the Western version of human rights, they advanced a conception of "the interdependence and indivisibility of economic, social, cultural, civil, and political rights" and suggested that "the promotion of human rights should be encouraged by cooperation and consensus, and not through confrontation and the imposition of incompatible values." Reprinted in *Human Rights and International Relations in the Asia Pacific,* ed. James Tang (London: Pinter, 1995), 204–5.

8. For a discussion of this diversity see Abdullahi A. An-Na'im, "Islamic Law, International Relations, and Human Rights: Challenge and Response," *Cornell International Law Journal* 20 (1987): 335.

9. Pheng Cheah claims that "existing human rights practices can be divided into three voices: what I will call the first voice is the position of governments in constitutional democracies in the economically hegemonic North or West. The second voice refers to the position of Asian governments. The third voice refers to the position of human rights NGOs in the South." "Posit(ion)ing Human Rights in the Current Global Conjecture," *Public Culture* 9 (1997): 8–9.

10. Statement by Wong Kan Seng, minister of foreign affairs of the Republic of Singapore, Vienna, June 16, 1993, entitled "The Real World of Human Rights," in Tang, *Human Rights,* 243.

11. For a useful discussion of these variations see Alison Dundes Renteln, "Relativism and the Search for Human Rights," *American Anthropologist* 90 (1988): 64. See also Alison Dundes Renteln, *International Human Rights: Universalism versus Relativism.* (London: Sage, 1990).

regularly violated by the some of the same governments that proclaim their adherence to human rights ideals.[12]

Nevertheless, appeals to human rights as a way of understanding and regulating the behavior of nations toward their people are as prevalent as they have ever been. "The past few decades," Richard Wilson notes, "have witnessed the inexorable rise of the application of international human rights law as well as the extension of a wider public discourse on human rights, to the point where human rights could be seen as one of the most globalized political values of our times."[13] This development is a result of the convergence of many factors, but perhaps none is more important than the demise of Communism and the ascendance of capitalism and liberal democracy throughout the world.

Democracy has replaced Marxism as "the hegemonic ideology of social change."[14] With the fall of Communism and the spread of democratization in Africa, Asia, and Latin America, the idea of rights has taken on new salience in political struggles in places where rights talk was formerly avoided or denigrated.[15] In the years since the end of World War II, Glendon argues,

> rights discourse has spread throughout the world. At the transnational level, human rights were enshrined in a variety of covenants

12. As Abdullahi A. An-Na'im puts it, "More than forty years after the adoption of the Universal Declaration of Human Rights in 1948, persistent and gross violations of fundamental human rights continue to occur in most parts of the world" (*Human Rights*, 1).

13. Richard Wilson, "Human Rights, Culture, and Context: An Introduction," in Wilson, *Human Rights*, 1.

14. Amrita Basu, "Social Movements, Globalization, and Human Rights: Perspectives from Asia," typescript, 1997, 8.

15. Jon Elster, "Constitutionalism in Eastern Europe," *University of Chicago Law Review* 58 (1991): 447. As Posner notes,
> Many of the Asian governments, like those of China and Singapore, that are most critical of U.S. human rights policy and seek to characterize it as Western-based and culturally biased are among the declining number of regimes that absolutely prevent any independent human rights group from operating. Their claims of cultural relativism can only be sustained if they continue to prevent their own people from raising human rights issues. But they are fighting a losing battle. Recent experience in countries as diverse as Chile, Kuwait, Nigeria, South Africa, and Sri Lanka leave no doubt that where people are allowed to organize and advocate their own human rights, they will do so. The common denominators in this area are much stronger than the cultural divisions.

Michael Posner, "Rally Round Human Rights," *Foreign Policy* 97 (1994–95): 137–38.

and declarations, notably the United Nations Universal Declaration of Human Rights. . . . At the same time, enumerated rights, backed up by some form of judicial review, were added to several national constitutions. . . . Nor was the rush to rights confined to "liberal" or "democratic" societies. American rights talk is now but one dialect in a universal language of rights.[16]

Commentators here and elsewhere worry that reliance on human rights in political struggles and by political movements invites a kind of legal imperialism, in which Western ideas and institutions take on an unhealthy prominence.[17] As the "rights industry" flourishes and the export of American ideas of rights grows dramatically, from abroad we hear claims that the spread of human rights is the latest manifestation of neocolonialism,[18] that it reflects a particularly insidious form of cultural imperialism. "The 'cultural' side," as Gary Peller explains, "reflects the notion that colonialism is not always imposed by visible material force nor according to the boundaries of formally constituted nation-states." "The 'imperialism' side," Peller continues, "embodies the understanding that disparate power is at issue."[19] Moreover, critics on both the political left and right attack rights as mystifying, alienating, and/or destructive of community.[20] At the very moment when

16. Mary Ann Glendon, *Rights Talk: The Impoverishment of Political Discourse* (New York: Free Press, 1991), 7.

17. See Pollis and Schwab, "Human Rights."

18. The debate at the Conference on International Human Rights in the summer of 1993 highlighted this critique. This debate illustrated the dialectic of nationalism and globalization in which national boundaries and traditions both are vehemently defended and, at the same time, give way to culture contact and the widespread circulation of images and ideas. In such an environment, does rights talk provide a global vocabulary that can respect local variation, or does the fact of globalization lose meaning if rights are adapted to the particular, the contingent, and the varied?

19. Gary Peller, "Cultural Imperialism, White Anxiety, and the Ideological Realignment of *Brown*," in *Race, Law, and Culture: Reflections on Brown v. Board of Education*, ed. Austin Sarat (New York: Oxford University Press, 1997), 193.

20. As Henkin notes,
From the perspective of some conceptions of the good society or the good life, the rights idea is selfish and promotes egoism. It is atomistic, disharmonious, confrontational, often litigious. . . . It is antisocial, permitting and encouraging the individual to set up selfish interests as he or she sees them against the common interest commonly determined. The idea of rights challenges democracy, negating popular sovereignty and frustrating the will of the majority. . . . The idea of rights, it is argued, is inefficient, tending to weaken society and render it ungovernable. Exalting rights de-emphasizes and breeds neglect of duties. It imposes an artificial and narrow view of the public good.

possibilities for realizing human rights seem particularly promising, one encounters questions about the fit between human rights and respect for cultural difference and the integrity of cultural traditions,[21] worries about whether human rights are, in truth culture-specific,[22] and doubts about the effectiveness of human rights in protecting subject populations from abuse.[23]

Yet democratic movements in many places continue to turn to human rights to legitimate their demands and advance their cause. For them the universalistic language of human rights is part of democracy's appeal, providing as it does the basis for connecting local struggles to global interests and for building alliances across national boundaries. That language provides at least a rhetorical counterweight to capitalist development in areas where the spread of capitalism threatens to exacerbate problems of dignity and equity.

The allure of human rights persists because they can, and do, mean many things at once.[24] Human rights can be sources of empowerment and protection for persons against the societies in which they live,[25] or they can constrain those same persons.[26] Additionally, they can liberate

---

Louis Henkin, *The Age of Rights* (New York: Columbia University Press, 1990), 182. See also Martin Golding, "The Primacy of Welfare Rights," *Social Philosophy and Policy* 1 (1984): 121, 124.

21. As Shute and Hurley note, "For contemporary liberal philosophers, the theory of human rights presents special problems that discourage straightforward engagement. Although liberal philosophers remain attached . . . to their individualist humanism, they are also sensitive to the allegation of cultural imperialism." Stephen Shute and Susan Hurley, eds., *On Human Rights: The Oxford Amnesty Lectures, 1993* (New York: Basic Books, 1993), 3. For a discussion of this concern see Teson, "International Human Rights."

22. Pannikar, "Notion of Human Rights."

23. See, for example, Diane Bell, "Considering Gender: Are Human Rights for Women, Too? An Australian Case," in An-Na'im, *Human Rights.*

24. As Cheah argues, "the open-ended nature of the human rights enterprise is expressed in the exhortatory nature of the *Declaration* (The Universal Declaration of Human rights) which involves a pledge by all signing nations to achieve a nonexhaustive common standard" ("Posit[ion]ing Human Rights," 10).

25. See David Richards, "Rights and Autonomy," 92 *Ethics* (1981): 3.

26. "[L]egal rights are interdependent and mutually defining. They arise in the context of relationships among people who are themselves interdependent and mutually defining. In this sense, every right and every freedom is no more than a claim limited by the possible claims of others. . . . Rather than expressions of some intrinsic autonomy, property rights announce complex, and often overlapping, relationships of individuals and the larger community to limited resources." Martha Minow, "Interpreting Rights: An Essay for Robert Cover," *Yale Law Journal* 96 (1987): 1884.

or limit the imagination of the possible;[27] they can revolutionize or con-
serve. Like all rights, international human rights authorize action and
yet undermine authority's claims. They are, by definition, mandatory
claims, yet they are fecund with interpretive possibilities.[28] They both
constitute us as subjects and provide a language through which we can
resist that constitution and forge new identities.[29]

The situation of human rights is, of course, all the more complicated when we take into account postcoloniality, the fact that formerly
colonized nations are now trying to develop new legal institutions and
new forms of state-society relations.[30] And, in a postcolonial world,
human rights claims can, and have been, mobilized against metropoli-
tan nations. Finally, the politics of human rights are by no means clear.
While they animate interstate relations, in some societies they have
become powerful tools used by social movements to mobilize opposition and resistance or to advance claims to legitimacy.[31]

Engaging with the theory and practice of human rights is, for the
student of law at the turn of the century, an especially inviting arena.
Here with unusual vividness and force some of the most important
debates in the field are being played out, debates in epistemology and
ethics, in hermeneutics and social theory. One turns to the subject of
human rights to learn about the genealogy of law and its association
with the production and reproduction of national power,[32] about the
meaning of culture and cultural variation as well as its significance for
law,[33] about rhetorical practices and political contests and the place of
rights in those practices and contests,[34] about globalization and its sig-

---

27. See Duncan Kennedy, "Critical Labor Law Theory: A Comment," *Industrial Relations Law Journal* 4 (1981): 503. Kennedy claims that rights "represent a liberating accom-
plishment of our culture" and that progressives do not "need a counter-theory that ends
with rights" (506).

28. See Minow, "Interpreting Rights."

29. Neal Milner, "The Denigration of Rights and the Persistence of Rights Talk: A
Cultural Portrait," *Law Social Inquiry* 14 (1989): 631.

30. On the significance of the postcolonial see Ian Chambers and Lidia Curti, eds.,
The Post-colonial Question: Common Skies, Divided Horizons (London: Routledge, 1996).

31. Margaret Keck and Kathryn Sikkink, *Activists without Borders: Transnational
Advocacy Networks in International Politics* (Ithaca: Cornell University Press, 1997).

32. See Peter Fitzpatrick, *The Mythology of Modern Law* (London: Routledge, 1992).

33. Rosemary Coombe, "Contingent Articulations: A Critical Cultural Studies of
Law," in *Law in the Domains of Culture,* ed. Austin Sarat and Thomas R. Kearns (Ann
Arbor: University of Michigan Press, 1998).

34. Merry, "Legal Pluralism."

nificance,[35] and about the way legal meanings are made and remade through the increasing, and increasingly unpredictable, play of local-global linkages.[36] The richness of these issues brings new generations of scholars to the subject of human rights and reenergizes those who have already made significant contributions to the field.

But all discussions of human rights must at some point or another engage the subject of rights themselves. In most discussions, whether or not they are framed as about international human rights, rights are assumed to be the entitlements of persons whose status as persons is fixed and from which rights are said to issue.[37] Rights-based theories *"presuppose* and protect the value of individual thought and choice."[38] The essential attributes of persons are, in this account, ahistorical and universal; as a result, humans are, in important ways, alike.[39] Human rights are said to be logically entailed by a recognition of those attributes. Thus, as Alan Gewirth argues, "Human rights are based upon and derivative from human dignity. It is because humans have dignity that they have . . . rights."[40] Or, as George Kateb puts it,

> Public and formal respect for rights registers and strengthens awareness of three . . . facts of being human: every person is a creature capable of feeling pain, . . . is a free agent capable of having a free being . . . , and is a moral agent capable of acknowledging that what one claims for oneself as a right one can claim only as an equal to everyone else. . . . Respect for rights recognizes these capacities and thus honors human dignity.[41]

35. See Michael Kearney, "The Local and the Global: The Anthropology of Globalization and Transnationalism," *Annual Review of Anthropology* 24 (1995): 547.

36. Coombe, "Contingent Articulations," 38–40.

37. A. I. Melden, *Rights and Persons* (Oxford: Basil Blackwell, 1977), chap. 6. See also Michael Meyer, "Dignity, Rights, and Self-Control," *Ethics* 99 (1989): 520. As Michael Perry puts it, "The idea of human rights . . . is that because every human being is, simply as a human being, sacred, certain choices should be made and certain choices rejected." *The Idea of Human Rights: Four Inquiries* (New York: Oxford University Press, 1998), 29.

38. Ronald Dworkin, *Taking Rights Seriously* (Cambridge: Harvard University Press, 1977), 172; emphasis added. See also Richards, "Rights and Autonomy."

39. See Perry, *Idea of Human Rights*.

40. See "Human Dignity as the Basis of Rights," in *The Constitution of Rights: Human Dignity and American Values*, ed. Michael Meyer and William Parent (Ithaca: Cornell University Press, 1992), 10. See also Joel Feinberg, "The Nature and Value of Rights," in *Rights, Justice, and the Bounds of Liberty* (Princeton: Princeton University Press, 1980), 151.

41. George Kateb, *The Inner Ocean: Individualism and Democratic Culture* (Ithaca: Cornell University Press, 1992), 5.

The second assumption in most theorizing about human rights is that rights stand outside of, and above, politics, where politics is understood as the play of group preferences or state policy. One makes appeals to rights as a defense against state policies, to hold them at bay. The force of these rights depends, so some argue, neither on the sentiments of electorates nor the desires of political elites. "The perspective of rights-based individualism," Kateb notes, "is suspicious of the political realm."[42] Human rights are, in this account, valuable since they entitle their holders willy-nilly to particular kinds of treatment. They provide an escape from the political realm because, in Dworkin's famous characterization, rights are "trumps."[43] If they are taken seriously, rights, including human rights, stop political argument and end political contest, and the recognition of a right removes the disputed claim from the political process. Thus, if taken seriously, rights make "the Government's job of securing the general benefit more difficult and more expensive."[44] Whenever such language is invoked, whenever someone says, "I have a right to something,"

> whether it is to exercise dominion over a possession, or enjoy equal employment opportunities, or express controversial opinions in public—I am not merely saying that I want to do it and hope others will let me; I am saying that they ought to let me, have a duty to let me, and will be guilty of an injustice, a transgression against established moral standards, if they fail to do so.[45]

The language of rights in general, and of human rights in particular, would seem to demand a grounding or foundation in something timeless and universal, something that establishes the transcultural and transhistorical basis of ethics and duty.[46] Yet today, many criticize the

---

42. Ibid., 25.

43. "Rights," Dworkin suggests, "are political trumps held by individuals. Individuals have rights when, for some reason, a collective goal is not sufficient justification for denying them what they wish, as individuals, to have or to do" (*Taking Rights Seriously*, xi).

44. Ibid., 198.

45. Thomas Haskell, "The Curious Persistence of Rights Talk in the 'Age of Interpretation,'" *Journal of American History* 74 (1987): 984. See also Jeremy Waldron, "A Right-Based Critique of Constitutional Rights," *Oxford Journal of Legal Studies* 13 (1993): 30.

46. Disputing this assertion, Richard Rorty argues that "one important intellectual advance made in our century is the steady decline in interest in the quarrel between Plato and Nietzsche. There is a growing willingness to neglect the question 'What is our nature?' and to substitute the question 'What can we make of ourselves?'" ("Human

search for the timeless, the universal, and the transcendent; at the same
time, they seek to hold onto the language of human rights.[47] Can they
have it both ways? Can they have human rights without foundations,
and, if so, at what price to rights themselves? As Jeremy Waldron
argues,

> Talk of . . . rights is often supposed to be a way of registering fairly
> basic objections to the arcane computations of the utilitarian calcu-
> lus. . . . The theorist of rights . . . is supposed to be the one who can
> produce the trump card, the peremptory argument stopper. . . .
> The idea of rights has often been seized on precisely as a way of
> avoiding the casuistry of trade-offs and complex moral calcula-
> tions. . . . The sad fact is, however, that this simplicity and moral
> certainty is simply unavailable. No one now believes that the truth
> about rights is self-evident or that, if two people disagree about
> rights, one of them at least must be either corrupt or morally
> blind.[48]

In addition to these philosophical criticisms of rights, the subject of
human rights raises difficult questions of historical interpretation.
What are the historical sources of these rights? When, and in what conditions, are new human rights imagined, and through what struggles
are they brought into being? Once brought into being what are their
limits? How can one reliably decide whether a human rights claim can
and should be honored?

These questions are, of course, not new. Contemporary criticism of

---

Rights, Rationality, and Sentimentality," in Shute and Hurley, *On Human Rights,* 115). For
a discussion of the question of the philosophical grounding of human rights see, for
example, John Rawls, "The Law of Peoples," in Shute and Hurley, *On Human Rights.*
Rawls puts it, "Basic human rights express a minimum standard of well-ordered political
institutions for all peoples who belong, as members in good standing, to a just political
society of peoples" (68).

47. Richard Rorty denounces what he calls "human rights foundationalism"
("Human Rights," 116).

48. Waldron, "Rights-Based Critique," 29. "It is no part of my theory," Dworkin
notes, "that any mechanical procedure exists for demonstrating what political rights,
either background or legal, a particular individual has. . . . [T]here are hard cases, both in
politics and at law, in which reasonable lawyers will disagree about rights, and neither
will have available any argument that must necessarily convince the other" (*Taking Rights
Seriously,* xiv).

human rights echoes Marx's warning that "the so-called rights of man ... are simply the rights of a member of civil society, that is, of egoistic man, of man separated from other men and from the community ... of man regarded as an isolated monad, withdrawn into himself."[49] Alternatively, it draws on Burke's denigration of abstract, sterile theorizing about "natural" or "universal" rights.[50] Echoing perhaps both Marx and Burke, contemporary critics insist that human rights cannot transcend the history of their creation and the interests and contexts out of which they develop.[51] They suggest that scholarly attention must be directed to particular rights claims in particular places at particular times.

On this conception, human rights do not define a unitary, universal human condition but designate rather a field of heterogeneous practices that help to constitute the array of subject moments or subject effects that comprise citizens and sovereigns. As a result, analysis must highlight both the context-specific qualities of rights and their constitutive effects.[52] Taking context into account means recognizing the contingent quality of, and the contingencies associated with, all rights.[53] As Neal Milner notes, rights are "demystified in this vision because the legal order's distinctiveness is minimized. If law cannot be separated from its social field, . . . [rights become] just another resource that can be used to convince others how to behave."[54] Examining their constitutive effects means inquiring into the way rights call into being, and enable, particular forms and expressions of personhood, as well as the

---

49. See Karl Marx, "On the Jewish Question," in *The Marx-Engels Reader,* ed. Robert Tucker (New York: Norton, 1972), 42.

50. Burke himself contrasted such rights with what he called the "real rights of men." Men, he argued,

> have a right to the fruits of their industry and to the means of making their industry fruitful. They have a right to the acquisitions of their parents, to the nourishment and improvement of their offspring, to instruction in life, and to consolation in death. Whatever each man can separately do, without trespassing upon others, he has a right to do for himself; and he has a right to a fair portion of all which society, with all its combinations of skill and force, can do in his favour.

Edmund Burke, *Reflections on the Revolution in France,* ed. J. G. A. Pocock (Indianapolis: Hackett, 1987), 51.

51. Rorty "Human Rights."

52. For a discussion of the constitutive effects of law and rights see Robert Gordon, "Critical Legal Histories," *Stanford Law Review* 36 (1984): 57.

53. Milner, "Denigration of Rights."

54. Ibid., 634.

way they disable others.[55] It means recognizing, as we have argued
elsewhere, that "Legal-thought and legal relations . . . dominate self-
understanding and one's understanding of one's relations to others.
. . . [W]e have internalized law's meanings and its representations of us,
so much so that our own purposes and understandings can no longer
be extricated from them."[56]

Always in the background of the debate about human rights is the
question of intervention. What right does one culture have to prescribe,
let alone impose, its values on another? What assumptions about culture and its meanings are inscribed in the call for human rights? How
can we both respect cultural difference and yet defend minimum standards to which all states must subscribe in the treatment of their citizens? For most scholars the answers to these questions are by no means
easy.[57] Many are tempted to embrace Appiah's view, that "we value
the variety of human forms of social and cultural life; we do not want
everybody to become part of a homogeneous global culture; and we
know that this means that there will be local difference . . . in moral cli-
mate as well. As long as these differences meet certain general ethical
constraints—as long, in particular, as political institutions respect basic
human rights—we are happy to let them be."[58] For those committed to
a cosmopolitan outlook and to the relief of human suffering,[59] the
rhetoric of human rights provides an attractive moral vocabulary, one
that supplies the grounding for political action irrespective of national

55. Neal Milner notes that "rights talk is one way people frame and assess their
worlds. . . . Because of their importance in American culture, rights play a powerful role
in both accommodation and resistance." "The Intrigues of Rights, Resistance, and
Accommodation," *Law and Social Inquiry* 17 (1992): 322, 330. See also Minow, "Interpreting Rights"; and Morton Horwitz, "Rights," *Harvard Civil Rights–Civil Liberties Law
Review* 23 (1988): 393.

56. Austin Sarat and Thomas R. Kearns, "Beyond the Great Divide: Forms of Legal
Scholarship and Everyday Life," in *Law in Everyday Life* (Ann Arbor: University of Michigan Press, 1993), 29.

57. One important, though ultimately unsatisfying, way of grappling with these
questions is found in the work of Michael Perry. As Perry argues, "Universalism about
human rights is correct: Human beings are alike in some respects, such that some things
good for some human beings are good for every human being and some things bad for
some human beings are bad for every human being. But pluralism about human good is
correct, too: There are many important respects in which human beings are not alike"
(*Idea of Human Rights*, 65).

58. Kwame Anthony Appiah, "Cosmopolitan Patriots," 23 *Critical Inquiry* (1997):
621.

59. See Martha Nussbaum, "Patriotism and Cosmopolitanism," *Boston Review*,
October–November, 1994, 3.

boundaries. Yet set against these possibilities are powerful arguments in favor of national self-determination and respect for the values and practices of historically marginalized peoples.[60]

These are old and continuing dilemmas. Nothing is likely to resolve them once and for all; nothing is likely to alleviate the anxiety generated when we confront morally repugnant practices embraced in places or among peoples with a very different idea of morality. Yet two new facts are, we think, transforming the context for thinking about human rights, facts that challenge conventional formulations and responses. The first is the fact of globalization, which radically reconfigures relations among nations, undoing the old center-periphery understanding of world relations;[61] the second is a new understanding of culture in which an awareness of internal plurality, fragmentation, and contestation replaces former tendencies to speak of cultures as if they were unified wholes.[62]

Globalization is by no means a totally new phenomena; what is new is its pace and intensification.[63] Globalization always involves the redistribution of power "outwards."[64] This is what Anthony Giddens calls the "intensification of worldwide social relations which link distant localities in such a way that local happenings are shaped by events occurring many miles away and vice versa."[65] As we see it, globalization is altering the context in which discussions of human rights occur and is, at the same time, reshaping what it means to talk about those rights.[66]

---

60. For a discussion of this tension in a different context see Peller, "Cultural Imperialism."

61. See Arjun Appadurai, *Modernity at Large: Cultural Dimensions of Globalization* (Minneapolis: University of Minnesota Press, 1996).

62. Coombe, "Contingent Articulations."

63. As Appadurai notes, "Today's world involves interactions of a new order and intensity. . . . With the advent of the steamship, the automobile, the airplane, the camera, the computer and the telephone, we have entered into an altogether new condition of neighborliness, even with those most distant from ourselves." Arjun Appadurai, "Disjuncture and Difference in the Global Cultural Economy," *Public Culture* 2 (1990): 1, 2.

64. Christopher Chase-Dunn, *Globalization: Structures of the World Economy* (Cambridge: Polity Press, 1991). As Seyla Benhabib notes, 'In the era of globalization, the integrative powers of the nation-state . . . are challenged." "Strange Multiplicities: Democracy and Identity in a Global Era: Lecture 1," typescript, 33.

65. Anthony Giddens, *The Consequences of Modernity* (Stanford, Calif.: Stanford University Press, 1990), 64.

66. Martin Shaw, "Civil Society and Global Politics: Beyond a Social Movements Approach," *Millennium* 23 (1992): 371.

At the material level, the outward redistribution of state power is seen in new suprastate organizations in Europe and North and Latin America. At the cultural level, it is seen in the penetration of even the most closed societies by common symbolic forms. "Rap music from American urban ghettos," Susan Silbey observes, " is played in the shops in Paris and on the streets in Budapest, portable telephones manufactured in Finland adorn the hips of stock brokers and manual laborers from Santiago to Sidney, from Cancún to Cape Town, and television stations around the globe fill their schedules with the likes of *Melrose Place* . . . while the office workers from Moscow to Buenos Aires munch on Big Macs and fries."[67] But the dispersion of common symbolic forms throughout the world does not entail a meaning shared everywhere. Common forms are reworked and remade through local idioms.[68] What is created is "the coexistence in a given space of several cultural traditions."[69] At the political level, outward redistribution of state power is seen in a kind of leveling out of intrastate differences, especially associated, on the one hand, with the ascendance of neoliberal values in a globalized economy, and, on the other, by similar, though by no means identical, patterns of cultural interpenetration, pluralization, and fragmentation.

All of these developments transform patterns of power within states, open up new possibilities of influence for forces seeking social change, and bring on new challenges. Globalization at once seems to provide a fertile terrain for the spread of human rights; yet it also reconfigures and intensifies patterns of privilege and disadvantage by further entrenching ideologies that legitimate a growing gap between rich and poor and, at the same time, decreasing rates of state investment in ameliorating those conditions.[70] Moreover, the insistent globalization of neoliberal practices and values can readily pit progressive elements in advanced capitalist societies and in modernizing countries against one another.

Cultural relativist arguments are, as Wilson notes, "increasingly

---

67. Susan Silbey, "'Let Them Eat Cake': Globalization, Postmodern Colonialism, and the Possibilities of Justice," *Law and Society Review* 31 (1997): 212.

68. Appadurai, *Modernity at Large.*

69. Richard Falk, "Cultural Foundations for the International Protection of Human Rights," in An-Na'im, *Human Rights,* 46.

70. Silbey, "Let Them Eat Cake."

undermined by the globalization of cultural, economic, and political processes and the increasingly convincing judgment that we are moving to a 'post-cultural' world."[71] In such a world it is hard to mark the boundaries where one culture and its moral values end and another begins. Moreover, globalization is not the same thing as westernization.[72] It involves a proliferation of diversity in which human rights norms, assumed to emanate in the traditions of one culture, are contested and decentered. Relations within, as well as among, nations are constructed out of "relatedness, opposition, and an awareness of plurality."[73]

In this context we need to rethink the traditional vocabularies of human rights: What is the meaning of self-determination? Of human dignity? Of choice for individuals and for cultures? We need to reconfigure the debate about universalism and relativism by moving away from an understanding of human rights that always juxtaposes the plurality of cultures and the alleged universal validity for moral norms.[74] As Appadurai puts it, "The central feature of global culture today is the politics of the mutual effort of sameness and difference to cannibalize one another and thus to proclaim their successful hijacking of the twin Enlightenment ideas of the triumphantly universal and the resiliently particular."[75]

In addition to globalization (and perhaps because of it), the understanding of culture and cultural integrity that has for so long been at the core of the debate about human rights is now being revised. The "com-

---

71. Wilson, "Human Rights," 10. Yet, as An-Na'im reminds us, "In this age of self-determination, sensitivity to cultural relativity is vital for the international protection and promotion of human rights. This point does not preclude cross-cultural moral judgment and action, but it prescribes the best ways of formulating and expressing judgment and of undertaking action." Abdullahi A. An-Na'im, "Toward a Cross-Cultural Approach to Defining International Standards of Human Rights: The Meaning of Cruel, Inhuman, or Degrading Treatment or Punishment," in *Human Rights*, 26.

72. "The globalization of culture is not the same as its homogenization" (Appadurai, "Disjuncture and Difference," 16).

73. Wilson, "Human Rights," 12.

74. For a fuller elaboration of this project see Cheah, "Posit(ion)ing Human Rights," 2. Cheah rightly suggests that "the question should not be whether universal human rights exist or not. Instead we should focus on the nature and limits of the normative claims being made by various actors . . . when they appeal to human rights within the theoretical framework of established human rights discourse" (4).

75. Appadurai, "Disjuncture and Difference," 17. For a less optimistic account of these developments see Liisa Malkki, "Citizens of Humanity: Internationalism and the Imagined Community of Nations," 3 *Diaspora* (1994): 41.

bined impact of technology, tourism, global capitalism, deterritorial-
ized communities, and migration are blurring and redrawing cultural
boundaries at a rapid rate."[76] Traditionally, discussion of human rights
has presumed the cultural integrity, if not homogeneity, of contending
forces, with those nations subscribing to human rights norms portrayed as in a hostile contest with those that did not. As Rosemary
Coombe notes, in the orthodox view, "cultures were depicted as holistic, integrated, and coherent systems of shared meaning."[77] As a result,
theorists could readily portray the arena of discussion of human rights
as "the West against the rest."[78] These portraits exacerbate debates
about universalism versus relativism, as if the only issue in the politics
of human rights was the grounds for outside intervention. Disputes
over human rights inevitably are treated as disputes at the level of contending nation-states; the activities of substate or nonstate actors
almost never come into view. As a result, contradictions, conflicts of
interest, and doubts about human rights or the policies allegedly in violation of human rights are ignored.[79]

Today we have a more complex view.[80] Neither domestic politics
nor culture itself is ever as stable and homogenized as the traditional
picture would have it.[81] The view of culture as static and homogeneous
is giving way in favor of a concept that sees culture as

> historically produced rather than static, unbounded rather than
> bounded and integrated, contested rather than consensual, incor-
> porated within structures of power. . . , rooted in practices, sym-
> bols, habits, patterns of practical mastery and practical rationality
> . . . , and negotiated and constructed through human action rather
> than superorganic forces."[82]

---

76. Appadurai, "Disjuncture and Difference," 6.

77. Coombe, "Contingent Articulations," 29.

78. Samuel Huntington, *The Clash of Civilizations and the Remaking of World Order*
(New York: Simon and Schuster, 1996).

79. Coombe, "Contingent Articulations," 30.

80. "Cultures are not homogeneous wholes: they are self-definitions and symbol-
izations which their members articulate in the course of partaking of complex social and
significative practices." Benhabib, "Strange Multiplicities: Democracy and Identity in a
Global Era: Lecture 2," typescript, 26.

81. See Ulf Hannerz, *Cultural Complexity*. (New York: Columbia University Press,
1992). Also Lila Abu-Lughood, "Writing against Culture," in *Recapturing Anthropology*,
Richard Fox, ed. (Sante Fe: School of American Research Press , 1991).

82. Sally Merry, "Law, Culture, and Cultural Appropriation," 10 *Yale Journal of Law
& the Humanities* (1998), 4.

This means that almost no practice of any political significance can be said to represent an entire culture's values. Rather nearly all practices are the subject of contest and struggle among groups within the culture and of dispute involving members of expatriate communities.[83]

Similarly, those who condemn a practice from the outside are unlikely to speak on behalf of a culture united in opposition. As Sally Merry notes,

> As long as cultures are seen as integrated, cohesive, bounded, and more or less static, it is simple to perceive human rights as an intrusive, alien discourse. However, recognizing that cultures are complex repertoires of systems of meanings extracted from myriad sources and reinterpreted through local understandings and interests provides a more fluid way of considering how human rights might be incorporated into local cultural practices and understandings.[84]

Moreover, we now know that political struggles over human rights may occur within nations as social movements seek change in the policies of domestic regimes.[85] Those movements use human rights claims to mobilize alliances within countries and across national borders.[86] Sometimes those claims are resisted by coalitions of national governments working in and through international organizations; sometimes movements are able to use those organizations to press their claims.

Taken together, these forces ensure that human rights are almost always contested in multiple and cross-cutting patterns and that their realization is variable and contingent. Attending to contestation and contingency as well as rethinking some of the basic concepts of human rights is the subject of the essays presented in *Human Rights: Concepts, Contests, Contingencies*. With the fact of globalization as well as cultural pluralization and fragmentation in the background, now is a good time to reappraise some of the key concepts in the debate over human rights

---

83. See Abdullahi Ahmed An-Na'im, "Toward a Cross-Cultural Approach to Defining International Standards of Human Rights: The Meaning of Cruel, Inhuman, or Degrading Treatment or Punishment," in *Human Rights in Cross-Cultural Perspectives*, 20.

84. Merry, "Legal Pluralism," 30.

85. Benhabib, "Strange Multiplicities," Lecture 2, 13.

86. In this context human rights politics often involve efforts to precipitate both *"internal cultural discourse and cross-cultural dialogue. . . .* This approach does not assume that sufficient cultural support for the full range of human rights is either already present or completely lacking in any given cultural tradition" (An-Na'im, *Human Rights*, 3).

as well as to begin to examine the contests and contingencies that shape the politics of human rights. Among the questions addressed in this book are the following: Can national self-determination be reconciled with human rights? Can human rights be advanced without thwarting efforts to develop indigenous legal traditions? How are the forces of modernization associated with globalization transforming our understandings of human dignity and personal autonomy? What does it mean to talk about culture and cultural choice? Is the protection of culture and cultural choice an important value in human rights discourse? How do human rights figure in local political contests and how are those contests, in turn, shaped by the spread of capitalism and market values? What contingencies shape the implementation of human rights in societies without a strong tradition of adherence to the rule of law? What are the conditions under which human rights claims are advanced and under which nations respond to their appeal?

Human Rights: Concepts, Contests, Contingencies brings together work by four noted scholars. The first two of these essays, by Iris Marion Young and Homi K. Bhabha, deal with basic conceptual issues in the vocabulary of human rights. The last two, by Jane F. Collier and Abdullahi A. An-Na'im, explore the contests and contingencies that shape the politics of human rights in Latin America and Africa. They analyze the national, subnational, and international factors that are in play as societies come to terms with particular human rights issues. Each of the essays in this book highlights the distinctive yet unsettled situation of human rights at the turn of the century.

We begin with Iris Young's "Two Concepts of Self-Determination," which takes up one of the most contested terms in the language of human rights, *self-determination.* Over time self-determination has taken on increasing importance as a norm in human rights. While neither the United Nations Charter nor the 1948 Declaration of Human Rights mentions a right of self-determination, international agreements of the last few decades have brought that right into greater prominence. Thus the Covenant on Economic, Social and Cultural Rights, the Covenant on Civil and Political Rights, and the Final Act of the Helsinki Conference on Security and Cooperation in Europe each affirms the right of a people to be free from external interference. Young notes that claims to self-determination proliferated during an earlier period of decolonization, and that it is invoked now in struggles over separation or secession in multiethnic states. Today this idea is both one of the internationally recognized centerpieces of human rights and a barrier to the achievement and implementation of others' rights. However, as Young sees it, this dilemma results from a particular way of thinking about self-determination, namely as a form or expression of what she labels "sovereign independence."

Young analyzes the situation of indigenous peoples, especially Native Americans in the United States, and shows that they have given a new meaning to the principle of self-determination.[87] "Indigenous peoples," she notes, "claim not to have full recognition of rights of self-determination." But they deny that a separate state is necessary for such recognition. How, Young asks, can we make sense of such a paradox and, in so doing, avoid the situation in which the principle of self-determination is used as an argument against other human rights?[88]

She answers this question by arguing for the need to reformulate our understanding of self-determination.[89] Traditionally this concept "interprets freedom as noninterference." However, Young suggests that that understanding is not adequate. Drawing on contemporary feminist and neorepublican political theory, she develops a "relational" account of self-determination that suggests that self-determination requires "nondomination" rather than noninterference. "Self-determination for peoples means that they have a right to their own governance institutions. . . . Other people ought not to constrain, dominate, or interfere . . . for the sake of their own ends, or according to their own judgment of what way of life is best." A self-determining people has a presumptive right to noninterference; they also have a right to make claims, negotiate the terms of their relationship, and mutually adjust their effects. Finally, such a people have the right, in Young's view, to participate in designing and implementing intergovernmental institutions aimed at minimizing domination.

87. Also see Benedict Kingsbury, "Claims by Non-state Groups in International Law," *Cornell International Law Journal* 25 (1992): 481.

88. For another way of thinking about this problem see Elizabeth Kiss, "Is Nationalism Compatible with Human Rights? Reflections on East-Central Europe," in *Identities, Politics, and Rights,* ed. Austin Sarat and Thomas R. Kearns (Ann Arbor: University of Michigan Press, 1995), 367.

89. See also Jürgen Habermas, "Human Rights and Popular Sovereignty: The Liberal and Republican Versions," *Ratio Juris* 7 (1994): 1.

But this does not mean that others have no claims on a self-determining people. Recognizing the pluralistic and fragmentary nature of culture, Young warns that self-determination cannot be used as a barrier to intergroup relations. Globalization, while not explicitly mentioned in Young's essay, brings greater contact among cultures and strengthens relationships. In this context, self-determination should be seen as a particular type of relationship, in which the various ways in which peoples are now tied together "oblige them to acknowledge the legitimate interests of others as well as promote their own."

From the language of self-determination we next move to Homi Bhabha's consideration of what he calls "cultural choice." Cultural choice combines ideas of self-determination, as in the idea of the choices that cultures make, and individual freedom, as in the idea that persons should have a right to choose their culture. It refers to "the freedom to choose a cultural affiliation, the right to be free to constitute or preserve a culture, or indeed to oppose it by exercising the moral 'right of exit.'" Like Young, Bhabha considers globalization and cultural fragmentation to be crucial in the contemporary situation of human rights. Transnational contexts of migration and complex multicultural overlays that unite supposedly disparate cultures provide the framework within which the question of choice must be examined. However, in Bhabha's view, these forces do not produce a uniform result. Bhabha rejects a linear story in which the forces of modernity triumph and produce an inevitable, if hard-fought, liberation.

Within Western nations the question of culture and choice is posed most vividly by so-called cultural defense cases. In those cases a member of a minority culture claims an exemption from prevailing legal norms on the basis that a practice otherwise condemned should be tolerated. Here the question of culture is vividly posed. Bhabha notes that those cases depend upon a reified, essentialized image of culture that, he contends, is neither descriptively accurate nor normatively desirable. But more crucial for the argument of this essay, those cases depend upon a particular image of agency and selfhood. It is to this image that Bhabha directs our attention.

Behind much of the discourse of human rights stands the image of, or desire for, a choosing subject. Through a reading of several texts in contemporary liberal thought, Bhabha asks us to rethink that image and that desire. Freedom, as liberals understand it, involves two things, not one, and both must be kept in view if we are to understand the politics of cultural choice. The first is the ability to form and act on one's own conception of the good; second is the ability to *revise* that conception over time. Thus "the freedom attributed to choice, within the liberal discourse, and the autonomous individual subject that subtends it, is only validated by the fact that a supplementary revisionary choice exists *belatedly after it, endowing it with its autonomy as a kind of delayed action, an afterwardness."*

By recognizing this supplement we can, Bhabha suggests, develop a different way of seeing the politics of human rights. Cultures do not just choose their values in a once-and-for-all manner. They are always in the shadowy presence of a revisionary moment or possibility. They have an "estranged relation to *themselves."* Bhabha argues for a new opening in the discourse of culture, choice, and rights, an opening to considerations of temporality and of temporal movement in the lives of all cultures. Those lives are as much about being "in between," about origin and revision, as they are about change from one situation to the other. No subject can be liberated from this in-betweenness, whether by her own act of choosing or by invocations of rights that supposedly exist outside of time. Individuals and cultures are always "uncannily confronted with [their] agonistic double." They are split against themselves in every act of choice and assertion.

Bhabha calls on his readers to "reconstitute the question of choice, to relearn the language of freedom" by focusing on "the middle, the *entre,* culture as a medium of betweenness." In this reconstitution and relearning, he contends, we may escape the binarism of self and other, universal and particular, that characterizes much of the contemporary human rights debate.

From reappraisals of self-determination, freedom, and choice brought on by globalization and cultural fragmentation, the last two essays move to context-specific considerations of the contests and contingencies that shape the lived reality (or absence) of human rights. The first step in that movement is provided by Jane Collier, whose essay is based on ethnographic fieldwork in Mexico and Spain. In this work Collier observed the breakdown of social systems in which prestige is found in the fulfillment of obligations to others. As the social systems she studied have been incorporated into the global capitalist system, selfish individualism has displaced the fulfillment of obligations as the basis of social status. This essay considers how human rights can be, and have been, used to ameliorate the conditions of "capitalist competition to actually create a world in which people enjoy . . . freedom from fear."

Collier begins with Durkheim. At the start of the twentieth century Durkheim tried to identify a moral discourse that would temper lais-sez-faire capitalism's celebration of amoral self-interest. Today, Collier suggests, human rights might provide one response to that effort. For example, the 1948 Universal Declaration of Human Rights actually articulates what Collier calls "a broad moral vision of the just society." But Collier is concerned as much with identifying the role human rights play in contestations at the local level as she is in grand theorizing about human rights. She calls on us to attend to the "economic and political contexts that shape whether and how appeals to human rights can help those most harmed by capitalism's impact."

Collier accepts the view that human rights are Western, but she thinks that in cultural and political contestation at the local level that "it is precisely because moral discourses of human rights and economic discourses of capitalism are both products of the post-Enlightenment West" that the former might effectively be enlisted against the latter. Moreover, the apparent tension between universalism and respect for cultural difference is itself one solely contained within Western dis-course. At the local level this tension does not inhibit action. Indige-nous groups make claims about human rights even as they reject the claim of human rights to universality. "In Chiapas, at least," she reports, "many people regard this tension between universalism and relativism as a productive one. They do not want to see it resolved in favor of either position."

Collier both celebrates the capacity of indigenous groups to mobi-lize under the banner of human rights and worries that "In the post–Cold War world, human rights commissions and state repression may be increasing together as the triumphant West, through interna-tional organizations, is requiring other states to simultaneously enact neoliberal economic reforms and to protect the civil and political rights of citizens." In this situation, abstract rights and international human rights organizations have not "produced a global system in which all people can live with dignity." If progress is to be made, it will be through local mobilization and appropriation of human rights con-cerns.

Yet, in the end, Collier is not optimistic. She worries that the forces of global capital will overwhelm such local mobilizations and, as a result, that "today . . . a young man [in Mexico] has good reason to wonder whether he might gain more advantage by investing his hard-earned money in capital goods such as a truck, or in prestige goods such as a television set or new cowboy boots, than in food and medicine for his wife and children."

The last essay, by Abdullahi A. An-Na'im, shifts the context but continues Collier's concern. Examining the implementation of human rights in postcolonial Africa, An-Na'im calls for a shift in emphasis from strategies of legal protection to local political mobilization. He argues that in the postcolonial situation the fate of human rights depends on the ability of local political actors to "do more . . . with less." Implementation, in his view, is highly contextual and contingent. It depends on a systematic and comprehensive response to structural, cultural, and other causes of violations.

An-Na'im suggests that while the promise of human rights was important in the creation of the postcolonial state in Africa, today post-colonial states remain so dependent on former colonial powers and so vulnerable within the system of global capitalism that they have achieved little in the way of genuine self-determination or protection of other human rights. Postcolonial states have reacted to their own weak-nesses and vulnerabilities by repressing dissent and treating political opponents like criminals. Nonetheless, like Young, An-Na'im does not see the push for self-determination as inevitably antithetical to the real-ization of other human rights. Instead, he claims, it focuses attention on local conditions and local strategies. He suggests that human rights constantly must be adapted to changing local conditions, lest they be little more than rhetorical devices with little ability to promote decent treatment for citizens.

Key to the implementation of human rights in postcolonial states are popular resistance and civil society activism. This is the case because "human rights have become associated with recolonization; emphasis on the legal protection of these rights is unable to check the massive violations that occur in the daily life of the vast majority of per-sons and groups who are subject to the jurisdiction of the postcolonial state in Africa." Popular resistance and civil society activism point away from law toward politics. Yet what a politics of human rights in Africa must face, An-Na'im concludes, is the fact that "addressing the root causes of human rights violations is an extremely complex and protracted task."

The essays in *Human Rights: Concepts, Contests, Contingencies* remind us of both the ascendance and fragility of human rights in an era of globalization and cultural fragmentation. They help us understand the resonance, and limits, of President Clinton's statements in China. They remind us that while the ideology of human rights is hegemonic, some of the basic concepts of that ideology are brought into question by the very conditions that promote its hegemony. And, at the local level, the results of the politics of human rights are far from certain. Does economic globalization reproduce at the international level the dilemma of liberalism in which rights are proclaimed but the material conditions for the equal dignity that they promise are simultaneously eroded? Can local activists enlist human rights in ways that address the structural causes of their violation? Or are the politics of human rights bound to recapitulate continuously a hopeful embrace of human aspiration as well as its regular defeat?

While few people today argue that the world would be a better place without those aspirations, no one can measure the extent to which it is made better by them. As Cheah reminds us, "Human rights are double-edged but absolutely necessary weapons that are given to the disenfranchised by the global force-relations in which they find themselves mired in a given historical conjuncture. . . . [H]uman rights are . . . not inevitably strategic or ideological instruments available for progressive or reactionary use. The normative force and effectivity that human rights have are given by the force-relations that make up the global capitalist system."[90] "Double-edged but absolutely necessary" is, we think, a fit characterization of the situation of human rights at the beginning of the twenty-first century as well as an apt invitation to scholars to reexamine and reappraise the concepts, contests, and contingencies that make human rights both meaningful and fragile.

---

90. Cheah, "Posit(ion)ing Human Rights," 31–32.

Two Concepts of Self-Determination

Iris Marion Young

In a speech before a 1995 meeting of the Open-Ended Inter-Sessional Working Group on Indigenous Peoples' Rights, established in accordance with the United Nations Commission on Human Rights, Craig Scott appealed to a meaning of self-determination as relationship and connection, not the commonly understood sense of separation and independence.

> If one listens, one can often hear the message that the right of a people to self-determination is not a right for peoples to determine their status without consideration of the rights of other peoples with whom they are presently connected and with whom they will continue to be connected in the future. For we must realize that peoples, no less than individuals, exist and thrive only in dialogue with each other. Self-determination necessarily involves engagement with and responsibility to others (which includes responsibility for the implications of one's preferred choices for others). . . . We need to begin to think of self-determination in terms of peoples existing in relationship with each other. It is the process of negotiating the nature of such relationships which is part of, indeed at the very core of, what it means to be a self-determining people.[1]

Scott does not develop a critical account of the concept of self-determination from which he distinguishes his own, nor does he explain the

I am grateful to David Alexander, Rainer Baubock, Augie Fleras, Philip Pettit, and Franke Wilmer for helpful comments on an earlier version of this essay.

1. Craig Scott, "Indigenous Self-Determination and Decolonization of the International Imagination: A Plea," *Human Rights Quarterly* 18 (1996): 819.

latter's meaning, justification, and implications. This essay takes up these tasks and argues for a relational approach along Scott's lines. My motive is to contribute to an understanding of the specific claims of indigenous peoples to self-determination. However, I believe that the concept of self-determination presented here applies to all peoples and relationships among peoples.

First I briefly review the current status of a principle of self-determination in international law and recent developments in views of indigenous peoples. Then I elaborate the historically prevailing interpretation of this principle, which continues to hold the minds of many who write on the subject. This interpretation equates self-determination with sovereign independence, a circumstance in which the self-determining entity claims a right of nonintervention and noninterference. Drawing particularly on feminist critiques of a concept of the autonomy of the person as independence and noninterference, I argue that this first concept of self-determination ignores the relations of interdependence peoples have with one another, especially in a global economic system. Again following the lead of feminist theories of autonomy, I argue for a relational concept of the self-determination of peoples. Philip Pettit's theory of freedom as *nondomination* indicates that peoples can be self-determining only if the relations in which they stand to others are nondominating. To ensure nondomination, their relations must be regulated both by institutions in which they all participate and by ongoing negotiations among them.

Self-Determination and International Politics

Neither the United Nations Charter nor the 1948 Declaration of Human Rights mentions a right of self-determination. General Assembly Resolution 1541 appears to be the origin of the post–World War II discourse of self-determination. Passed with the project of decolonization in view, the resolution defines self-government as entailing either independence, free association with an independent state, or the integration of a people with an independent state on the basis of equality. It implicitly entails the "saltwater" test for ascertaining whether a people deserves recognition of their right to ˙self-determination, that is, whether they have a distinct territory separated by long global distances from a colonial power from which they claim independence. Recognition of self-determination in these cases entails recognition of separate independent sovereign states if that is what the former colonies wish.

Between the era of postcolonial independence and the early 1990s the international community showed great reluctance to apply a principle of self-determination to disputes among peoples in territorial contiguity. In two decades fewer than ten new states were established and recognized under such a principle. As international law on human rights has evolved, some scholars have argued that many issues of freedom and self-governance can be treated under principles of individual human rights, without invoking a collective principle of self-determination—such as rights of minorities against discrimination and persecution, rights to participate in the governance of the state, and rights of cultural practice and preservation.

Some international agreements since the 1950s, however, elaborate further a principle of self-determination for peoples. The Covenant on Economic, Social and Cultural Rights and Covenant on Civil and Political Rights, which were drafted in 1966 and went into force in 1976, state such a principle in Article 1. All peoples have the right to self-determination, which means freely to determine their political status and pursue economic, social, and cultural development. The Helsinki Final Act of 1975, the Conference on Security and Cooperation in Europe, also reaffirms the right of a people to be free from external influence in choosing their own form of government.[2]

A principle of self-determination, then, has been increasingly recognized as applying to all peoples, and not only those in the territories of the former European colonies of Africa and Asia. Continued and wider affirmation of a principle of self-determination in international documents encourages indigenous groups and other displaced, oppressed, or dominated groups to press claims against states that assert jurisdiction over them both directly and in international forums. Hotly contested, of course, is just what counts as a "people" who have a legitimate claim to self-determination. This crucial question cannot be settled by a fixed definition. Peoples are not natural kinds, clearly identifiable and distinguishable by a set of essential attributes. Although I

---

2. On the state of international law, see Hurst Hannum, "Self-Determination in the Post-Colonial Era," in *Self-Determination: International Perspectives*, ed. Donald Clark and Robert Williamson (New York: St. Martin's Press, 1996), 12–44; see also Hannum, *Autonomy, Sovereignty, and Self-Determination: The Accommodation of Conflicting Rights* (Philadelphia: University of Pennsylvania Press, 1990).

shall not argue this here, the relations among peoples and their degrees of distinctness are more fluid, relational, and dependent on context than such a substantial logic suggests.[3]

Instead of addressing the important and contentious question of what a people is, here I will assume that there are groups in the world today whose status as distinct peoples is largely uncontested, but who do not have states of their own and make claims for greater self-determination. Among such groups are at least some of those called indigenous peoples.

I bracket the question of what is a people in order to focus on self-determination. For while a principle of self-determination has acquired a wider scope in international law in recent decades, it has lost conceptual clarity and precision. Since the era when former colonies obtained state independence, the international community has been very reluctant to allow a principle of self-determination to ground or endorse claims of separation, secession, and the formation of new states. The breakup of the Soviet Union and Yugoslavia into separate sovereign states is a grand exception, largely explicable by a cynical desire in the West to weaken a former world power. Claims by minority groups that they are wrongly subordinated by dominant groups in nation-states seem to be getting more hearing in international political discussions. At the same time global powers give a strong priority to the preservation of existing state territories. Thus scholars and practitioners of international law widely hold that if certain peoples have rights to self-determination, possessing them does not entail rights to secede from existing nation-states and establish their own sovereign states with exclusive rights over a contiguous territory. However, such clarity on what self-determination does not imply produces confusion about what it does imply. It this question that I address by means of theoretical arguments both moral and political.

The Claims of Indigenous Peoples

For more than twenty years United Nations commissions have met to discuss the claims and status of the world's indigenous peoples. This

---

3. I develop some of this argument in another essay, "Self-Determination and Global Democracy: A Critique of Liberal Nationalism," in *Designing Democratic Institutions: Nomos XLII*, ed. Ian Shapiro and Stephen Macedo (New York: New York University Press, 2000); see also I. M. Young, *Inclusion and Democracy* (Oxford: Oxford University Press, 1990).

work culminated in the UN Draft Declaration of the Rights of Indigenous Peoples, discussed at the meeting in 1995 to which Scott addressed his plea. Indigenous activists hope that this declaration or a close sister will be approved by a majority of the world's states and peoples by the end of the UN Decade on the Indigenous in 2004.[4]

At issue in world forums and in documents such as the draft declaration are both the definition of indigenous peoples and the identification of groups to whom it applies. Just who counts as indigenous is fairly clear in the case of the settler colonies of the Americas, Australia, and New Zealand. They are the people who inhabited the land for centuries before the European settlers came, and who live today in some continuity with the premodern ways of life of their ancestors. The United Nations, however, also recognizes some other peoples in Europe, Asia, and Africa as indigenous, a designation that some states contest for some of "their" minorities. Still other groups that the United Nations does not recognize as indigenous would like to be so recognized. Just who should and should not count as indigenous people, as distinct from simply ethnic groups, is a contentious issue. Although this question is also important, I will bracket it as well. I will assume that descendants of the pre-Columbian inhabitants of North and South America count as indigenous people, as well as the Aboriginal people of New Zealand and Australia. While I believe there are others who ought to have rights of indigenous people, in this essay I will not develop or apply criteria for classifying a people as indigenous. I begin by reflecting on the claims of (at least some) indigenous people, but ultimately the conception of self-determination that I recommend ought to apply to all peoples. Thus for the argument of this essay it is necessary neither to find an iron-clad definition of *indigenous* nor to sort out which peoples fit it.

The UN draft declaration specifies that indigenous peoples have a right to autonomy or self-government in matters relating to their internal and local affairs, including culture, employment, social welfare, economic activities, land and resources, management, and environment.[5] Nothing in the declaration implies that indigenous peoples have

---

4. See Russell Lawrence Barsh, "Indigenous Peoples and the U.N. Commission on Human Rights: A Case of the Immovable Object and the Irresistible Force," *Human Rights Quarterly* 18 (1996): 782–813.

5. Erica-Irene A. Daes, "The Right of Indigenous Peoples to Self-Determination in the Contemporary World Order," in Clark and Williamson, *Self-Determination,* 55.

a right to form separate states, and few if any seek to do so. Most seek explicit recognition as distinct peoples by the states that claim to have jurisdiction over them, and wider terms of autonomy and negotiation with those states and with the other peoples living within those states. They claim or seek significant self-government rights, not only with respect to cultural issues, but with respect to land and access to resources. They claim to have rights to be distinct political entities with which other political entities, such as states, must negotiate agreements and over which they cannot simply impose their will and their law.

Although indigenous peoples rarely seek to be separate states, they nevertheless claim that their legitimate rights of self-determination are nowhere completely recognized and respected. Every region of the world has its own stories and struggles of indigenous peoples in relation to the states that have emerged from colonization, and a full review of these claims and struggles would take me away from the conceptual work that is the main task of this essay. Thus I will focus on the example of indigenous peoples related to the United States. Native Americans have a relatively long history of institutions of self-government recognized by the United States government; in the last twenty years Native self-government has been more actual than ever before. Nevertheless, Native Americans typically claim that the United States government has never recognized their rights to self-determination, and that they are not so recognized today. Congress reserves the right to recognize a group as a tribe, a status that accords it self-government rights. Congress believes itself to have the power to rescind tribal status at any time, and it has done so in the past, most notably during the period in the 1950s when the Indian Termination Act was in effect. Congress continues to act as though it has ultimate legislative authority over Native Americans. In the Indian Gaming Act of 1988, Congress for the first time required Native peoples to negotiate with state governments regarding the use of Indian lands.

Some U.S. public officials believe that Indians should not have distinct and recognized self-government and legal jurisdiction, and have led efforts to cripple Indian sovereignty. In the most recent attack, in fall 1997, Senator Slade Gorton (R–Washington) led a move to make the allocation of funds to tribal governments conditional on their waiving their current immunity from civil lawsuits filed in United States courts. This effort, hidden within the bill allocating funds to the National Endowment for the Arts and for national parks, was defeated. Even if it had passed it would likely not have stood up to treaty-based court challenge. It nevertheless shows how thin the line may be between self-government and subjection for Native Americans today.

The process of rethinking the concept of the self-determination of peoples begins from this apparent paradox. Indigenous peoples claim not to have full recognition of rights of self-determination, but most do not claim that establishing separate states is necessary for such recognition. The prevailing contemporary meaning of self-determination seems to require sovereign statehood. What, then, is a concept of self-determination that corresponds to the claims of indigenous peoples? I will argue that self-determination as relational autonomy in the context of nondomination best corresponds to their claims.

Self-Determination as Noninterference

Although international political and legal developments of recent decades have brought it into question, the most widely accepted and clearly articulated meaning of self-determination is independent *sovereignty.* An authority is sovereign, in this sense, when it has final say over the regulation of all activities within a territory, and when no entity outside that territory has the legitimate right to cancel or override its determinations.[6]

This concept of self-determination interprets freedom as noninterference. On this model, self-determination means that a people or government has the authority to exercise complete control over what goes on inside its jurisdiction, and no outside agent has the right to make claims upon or interfere with what the self-determining agent does. Reciprocally, the self-determining people has no claim on what others do with respect to issues within their jurisdictions, and no right to interfere in others' business. Just as it denies rights of interference by outsiders in a jurisdiction, this concept assumes that each self-determining entity has no inherent obligations to outsiders.

Only states have a status approaching self-determination as noninterference in today's world. When the principle of self-determination was systematized in the early twentieth century and then again after World War II, world leaders created or authorized the formation of states according to criteria of viability and independence. To be sover-

6. See Thomas Pogge, "Cosmopolitanism and Sovereignty," *Ethics* 103 (October 1992): 48–75.

eign or self-determining and thus to have a right of noninterference, a state, it was thought, must be large enough to stand against other states if necessary and have the resources to thrive economically without depending on outsiders. Thus the world powers that created states after World War I were concerned that no state be landlocked and that states recognized as sovereign have sufficient natural resources to sustain an independent economy. The powers creating states in the decades after World War II also brought these standards of viability for independent living to bear on their work, usually seeking to make states large, though they did not always succeed in doing so. Some theorists who are reluctant to apply a principle of self-determination continue to make the capacity for economic independence a condition of such exercise of self-determination.

Some political theorists argue that state sovereignty considered as final authority and the enjoyment of noninterference is eroding, and may have never existed to the extent that concept supposes.[7] Some think that global capitalism and international law increasingly circumscribe the independence and sovereignty of states.[8] Here I am less concerned with whether any peoples or governments actually have self-determination as noninterference, however, than with evaluating the normative adequacy of the concept, especially in light of indigenous peoples' claims. I argue in what follows that noninterference is not a normatively adequate interpretation of a principle of self-determination. My discussion relies on two different but compatible efforts to theorize a concept of individual autonomy that criticize the primacy of noninterference and offer alternative accounts. The first comes from feminist political theory, the second from neorepublican theory. Both suggest that freedom as noninterference does not properly take account of social relationships and possibilities for domination. Their arguments can be extended from relations among individuals to relations among peoples.

Freedom as noninterference presupposes that agents have their own domain of action independent of any need for relationship with, or influence by, others. The status of autonomous citizenship presup-

---

7. See Daniel Philpott, "Sovereignty: An Introduction and Brief History," *Journal of International Affairs* 48, no. 2 (winter 1995): 353–68.

8. See David Held, *Democracy and the Global Order* (Oxford: Polity Press, 1995), chaps. 5 and 6; Ruth Lapidoth, "Sovereignty in Transition," *Journal of International Affairs* 45, no. 2 (winter 1992): 325–46.

poses this private sphere of individual property. From this base of independence individual agents enter relationships with others through voluntary agreements. Except where obligations are generated through such agreements, the freedom of individuals ought not to be interfered with unless they are directly and actively interfering with the freedom of others. The ideal of self-determination, on this view, consists in an agent's being left alone to conduct his or her affairs in his or her own independent sphere.

Critics of liberal individualism since Hegel have argued that this image of the free individual as ontologically and morally independent fails to recognize that subjects are constituted through relationships, and that agents are embedded in institutional relations that make them interdependent in many ways. Relational feminist critics of the equation of freedom with noninterference draw on both these insights. In contrast to a subject constituted through bounding itself from others, a relational account proposes that the individual person is constituted through communicative and interactive relations with others. The individual acquires a sense of self from being recognized by others with whom she has relationships; she acts in reference to a complex web of social relations and social effects that both constrain and enable her.[9]

On this account, the idea that a person's autonomy consists in control over a domain of activity independent of others and from which they are excluded except through mutual agreements is a dangerous fiction. This concept of self-determination as noninterference values independence and thereby devalues any persons not deemed independent by its account. Historically, this meant that only property-holding heads of household could expect to have their freedom recognized. Women and workers could not be fully self-determining citizens because their position in the division of labor rendered them depen-

---

9. See Anna Yeatman, "Beyond Natural Right: The Conditions for Universal Citizenship," in *Postmodern Revisionings of the Political* (New York: Routledge, 1994), 57–79, "Feminism and Citizenship," in *Cultural Citizenship,* ed. Nick Stevenson (London: Sage, 1998), and "Relational Individualism," typescript; see also Jennifer Nedelsky, "Relational Autonomy," in *Yale Women's Law Journal* 1, no. 1 (1989), 7–36; and "Law, Boundaries, and the Bounded Self," in *Law and the Order of Culture,* ed. Robert Post (Berkeley: University of California Press, 1991); for an application of this feminist revision of autonomy to international relations theory see Karen Knop, "Re/Statements: Feminism and State Sovereignty in International Law," *Transnational Law and Contemporary Problems* 3, no. 2 (fall 1993): 293–344; see also Jean Elshtain, "The Sovereign State," *Notre Dame Law Review* 66 (1991): 1355–84.

dent on the property holders. Feminist criticism argues, however, that in fact the male head of household and property holder is no more independent than the women or workers he rules. The appearance of his independence is produced by a system of domination in which he is able to command and benefit form the labor of others. This frees him from bodily and menial tasks of self-care and routine production and helps increase his property, so that he can spend his time at politics or business deals. In fact the more powerful agents are as embedded in interdependent social relations as the less powerful agents. Feminists argue that contemporary discourse of the freedom of individuals understood as noninterference continues to assume falsely that all or most persons are or ought to be independent in the sense that they need nothing from others and can rely on their own sphere of activity to support them.

Feminist theory thus offers an alternative concept of autonomy that takes account of the interdependence of agents and their embeddedness in relationships at the same time that it continues to value individual choices. In this concept, all agents are owed equal respect as autonomous agents, which means that they are able to choose their ends and have the capacity and support to pursue those ends. They are owed this respect because they are agents, not because they inhabit a sphere separate from others. The social constitution of agents and their acting in relations of interdependence mean the ability to be separate from others is rare, if it happens at all. Thus an adequate conception of autonomy should promote the capacity of individuals to pursue their own ends in the context of relationships in which others may do the same. While this concept of autonomy entails a presumption of noninterference, especially with the choice of ends, it does not imply a social scheme in which atomized agents simply mind their own business and leave each other alone. Instead, it entails recognizing that agents are related in many ways they have not chosen, by virtue of kinship, history, proximity, or the unintended consequences of action. In these relationships agents are able either to thwart or to support one another. Relational autonomy consists partly, then, in the structuring of relationships so that they support the maximal pursuit of individual ends.

In his reinterpretation of ideals of classical republicanism, Philip Pettit offers a similar criticism of the idea of freedom as noninterference.[10] Interference means that one agent blocks or redirects the action

---

10. Philip Pettit, *Republicanism* (Oxford: Oxford University Press, 1997).

of another in a way that worsens that agent's choice situation by changing the range of options. On Pettit's account, noninterference, while related to freedom, is not equivalent to it. Instead, freedom should be understood as nondomination. An agent dominates another when he or she has power over that other and is thus able to interfere with the other *arbitrarily*. Interference is arbitrary when it is chosen or rejected without consideration of the interests or opinions of those affected. An agent may dominate another, however, without ever interfering with that person. Domination consists in standing in a set of relations that makes an agent *able* to interfere arbitrarily with the actions of others.

Thus freedom is not equivalent to noninterference both because an unfree person may not experience interference, and because a free person may be interfered with. In both cases the primary criterion of freedom is nondomination. Thus when a person has a personal or institutional power that makes him or her able to interfere with my action arbitrarily, I am not free, even if in fact the dominating agent has not directly interfered with my actions. Conversely, a person whose actions are interfered with for the sake of reducing or eliminating such relations of domination is not unfree. On Pettit's account, it is appropriate for governing agents to interfere in actions in order to promote institutions that minimize domination. Interference is not arbitrary if its purpose is to minimize domination, and if it is done in a way that takes the interests and voices of affected parties into account. Like the feminist concept of relational autonomy, then, the concept of freedom as nondomination refers to a set of social relations. "Non-domination is the position that someone enjoys when they live in the presence of other people and when, by virtue of social design, none of those others dominates them" (67).

In sum, both the feminist and neorepublican criticisms of the identification of freedom with noninterference are mindful of the relations in which people stand. A concept of freedom as noninterference aims to buffer the agent from those relations and imagines an independent sphere of action unaffected by, and not affecting, others. However, because persons and groups are deeply embedded in relationships, many of which they have not chosen, they do affect one another in their actions, even when they do not intend this mutual effect. Such interdependence is part of what enables domination, the ability for some to interfere arbitrarily with the actions of others. Freedom, then, means regulating and negotiating relationships so that all persons are able to be secure in the knowledge that their interests, opinions, and desires for action are taken into account.

Relational Interpretation of Self-Determination

We are now in a position to fill out Scott's claim that we should think of the self-determination of peoples in the context of relationships. For the moment the discussion focuses on the situation of indigenous people in the Americas and the antipodes. Because of a long and dominative history of settlement, exchange, treaty, conquest, removal, and sometimes recognition, indigenous and nonindigenous peoples are now interrelated in their territories. Webs of economic and communicative exchange, moreover, place the multicultural peoples of a particular region in relations of interdependence with others far away. In such a situation of interdependence, it is difficult for a people to be independent in the sense that they require nothing from outsiders and their activity has no effect on others.

I propose that the critique of the idea of freedom as noninterference and an alternative concept of relational autonomy and nondomination is not only relevant to thinking about the meaning of freedom for individuals. It can be usefully extended to an interpretation of the self-determination of a people. Extending any ideas of individual freedom and autonomy to peoples, of course, raises conceptual and political issues of what is the "self" of a people analogous to individual will and desire, by which it can make sense to apply a concept of self-determination to a people at all. Extending political theoretical concepts of individual freedom to a people appears to reify or personify a social aggregate as a unity with a set of common interests, agency, and will of its own.[11] In fact, however, no such unified entity exists. Any tribe, city, nation, or other designated group is a collection of individuals with diverse interests and affinities, prone to disagreements and internal conflicts. One rarely finds a set of interests agreed upon by all members of a group that can guide their autonomous government. When we talk about self-determination for a people, moreover, we encounter the further problem that it is sometimes ambiguous who belongs to a particular group, and that many individuals have reasonable claim to belong to more than one. Since a group has neither unanimity nor bounded unity of membership, what sense does it make to recognize its right to self-determination?

It is certainly true that group membership is sometimes plural, ambiguous, and overlapping, and that groups cannot be defined by a single set of shared attributes or interests. This is why it is sometimes

---

11. See Russell Hardin, *One for All* (Chicago: University of Chicago Press, 1995), for a critique of the notion of collective common interests in the context of nationalist politics.

difficult to say decisively that a particular collection of individuals counts as a distinct people. Such difficulties do not negate the fact, however, that historical and cultural groups have often been and continue to be dominated and exploited by other groups who often use state power to do so. Nor do these ambiguities negate the fact that freedom as self-government and cultural autonomy is important to many persons who consider themselves belonging to distinct peoples.

Any collection of persons that constitutes itself as a political community must respond to conflict and dissent within the community, and determine whether the decisions and actions carried out in the name of a group can be said to *belong* to the group. For this reason the "self" of a group that claims a right to self-determination needs more explication than does the "self" of individual persons, though the latter concept is hardly clear and distinct. Insofar as a collective has a set of institutions through which that people make decisions and implement them, then the group sometimes expresses unity in the sense of agency. Whatever conflicts and disagreements may have led up to that point, once decisions have been made and action taken through collective institutions, the group itself can be said to act. Such a discourse of group agency and representation of agency to wider publics need not falsely personify the group or suppress differences among its members. Most governments claim to act for "the people," and their claims are more or less legitimate to the extent that the individuals in the society accept the government and its actions as theirs, and even more legitimate if they have had real influence in its decision-making processes. This capacity for agency is the only secular political meaning that the "self" of collective self-determination can have.

Self-determination for indigenous peoples, as well as other peoples, should not mean noninterference. The interpretation of self-determination modeled on state sovereign independence equates a principle of self-determination with noninterference. For the most part indigenous peoples do not wish to be states in that sense, and while they claim autonomy, they do not claim such a blanket principle of noninterference. Their claims for self-determination, I suggest, are better understood as a quest for an institutional context of nondomination.[12]

---

12. For one effort toward this sort of conceptualization in the context of the relation of Maori and Pakeha in New Zealand, see Roger Maaka and Augie Fleras, "Politicizing Customary Rights: Tino Rangatirantanga and the Politics of Engagement," paper presented to the Conference on Indigenous Rights, Political Theory, and the Reshaping of Institutions, Australian National University, Canberra, August 1997.

On such an interpretation, self-determination for peoples means that they have a right to their own governance institutions through which they decide on their goals and interpret their way of life. Other people ought not to constrain, dominate, or interfere with those decisions and interpretations for the sake of their own ends, or according to their judgment of what way of life is best, or in order to subordinate a people to a larger "national" unit. Peoples, that is, ought to be free from domination. Because a people stands in interdependent relations with others, however, a people cannot ignore the claims and interests of those others when their actions potentially affect them. Insofar as outsiders are affected by the activities of a self-determining people, those others have a legitimate claim to have their interests and needs taken into account even though they are outside the government jurisdiction. Conversely, outsiders should recognize that when they themselves affect a people, the latter can legitimately claim that they should have their interests taken into account insofar as they may be adversely affected. Insofar as their activities affect one another, peoples are in relationship and ought to negotiate the terms and effects of the relationship.

Self-determining peoples morally cannot do whatever they want without interference from others. Their territorial, economic, or communicative relationships with others generate conflicts and collective problems that oblige them to acknowledge the legitimate interests of others as well as promote their own. Pettit argues that states can legitimately interfere with the actions of individuals in order to foster institutions that minimize domination. A similar argument applies to actions and relations of collectivities. In a densely interdependent world, peoples require political institutions that lay down procedures for coordinating action, resolving conflicts, and negotiating relationships.

The self-determination of peoples, then, has the following elements. First, self-determination means a presumption of noninterference. A people has the prima facie right to set its own governance procedures and make its own decisions about its activities, without interference from others. Second, insofar as the activities of a group may adversely affect others, or generate conflict, self-determination entails the right of those others to make claims on the group, negotiate the terms of their relationships, and mutually adjust their effects. Third, a world of self-determining peoples thus requires recognized and settled institutions and procedures through which peoples negotiate, adjudicate conflicts, and enforce agreements. Self-determination does not imply independence, but rather peoples dwelling together within political institutions that minimize domination among peoples. (It would take another essay to address the question of just what form such intergovernmental political institutions should take; some forms of federalism do and should apply.) Finally, the self-determination of peoples requires that they have the right to participate *as peoples* in designing and implementing intergovernmental institutions aimed at minimizing domination.

I have argued for a principle of self-determination understood as relational autonomy in the context of nondomination, as opposed to a principle of self-determination understood as simple noninterference. This argument applies as much to large nation-states as to small indigenous groups. Those entities that today are considered self-determining independent states in principle ought to have no more right of noninterference than should smaller groups. Self-determination for those entities now called sovereign states should mean nondomination. While this means a presumption of noninterference, outsiders may have a claim on their activities.

Understanding freedom as nondomination implies shifting the idea of state sovereignty into a different context. Sovereign independence is neither a necessary nor a sufficient condition of self-determination understood as nondomination. A self-governing people need not be able to say that it is entirely independent of others in order to be self-determining; indeed, I have argued that such an idea of independence is largely illusory. For these reasons self-governing peoples ought to recognize their connections with others and make claims on others when the actions of those others affect them, just as the others have a legitimate right to make claims on them when their interdependent relations threaten to harm them.

Those same relations of interdependence mean, however, that sovereign independence is not a sufficient condition of self-determination understood as nondomination. The peoples living within many formally independent states stand in relation to other states, or powerful private actors such as multinational corporations, where those others are able to interfere arbitrarily with the peoples in order to promote their own interests. For some peoples formal sovereignty is little protection against such dominative relations. The institutions of formal state sovereignty, however, allow many agents to absolve themselves of responsibility to support self-governing peoples who nevertheless stand in relations of domination.

Thus the interpretation of self-determination as nondomination ultimately implies limiting the rights of existing nation-states and setting them into more cooperatively regulated relationships. Just as promoting freedom for individuals involves regulating relationships in order to prevent domination, so promoting self-determination for peoples involves regulating international relations to prevent domination.

Applying a principle of self-determination as nondomination to existing states, then, as well as to peoples not currently organized as states, has profound implications for the freedom of the former. States ought not to have rights to interfere arbitrarily in the activities of those peoples in relation to whom they claim special jurisdictional relation. In the pragmatic context of political argument within both nation-state and international politics, many indigenous groups do not deny that their rights of autonomy must fit within the framework of nation-states. Some appear to recognize that nation-states presume a right of noninterference in dealings with "their" autonomous minorities.[13] If self-determination for peoples means not noninterference but nondomination, however, then nation-states cannot have a right of noninterference in their dealings with indigenous minorities and other ethnic minorities. Small, resource-poor, relatively weak peoples are most likely to experience domination by larger and more organized peoples living next to or among them than by others far away. The nation-state that claims jurisdiction with respect to a relatively autonomous people is likely sometimes to dominate that people. If a self-determining people has no public forum in which to press claims of such wrongful domination against a nation-state, and if no agents outside the state have the authority and power to affect a state's relation to that people, then that people cannot be said to be self-determining.

Thus a principle of self-determination for indigenous peoples can have little meaning unless it accompanies a limitation on and ultimately a transformation of the rights and powers of existing nation-states and the assumptions of recognition and noninterference that still largely govern the relation between states.[14] There are good reasons to

13. See, for example, Hector Diaz Polanco, *Indigenous Peoples in Latin America: The Quest for Self-Determination,* trans. Lucia Rayas (Boulder, Colo.: Westview Press, 1997), especially part 2.

14. See Franke Wilmer, *The Indigenous Voice in World Politics* (London: Sage, 1993).

preserve the coordination capacities that many existing states have and to strengthen these capacities where they are weak. Nevertheless, the capacities of diverse peoples to coordinate action to promote peace, distributive justice, or ecological value can in principle be maintained and enlarged within institutions that also aim to minimize the domination that states are able to exercise over individuals and groups.

Illustration: The Goshutes versus Utah

Let me illustrate the difference between self-determination as noninterference and self-determination as autonomy in regulated relations by reflecting on a particular conflict between a Native American tribe and some residents of Utah.

According to a report in the *New York Times*,[15] the Skull Valley Band of Goshutes has offered to lease part of their reservation as the temporary storage ground for high-level civil nuclear waste. The State of Utah's territory surrounds this small reservation, and state officials have vowed to block the border of the reservation from shipments of nuclear waste. The Skull Valley Band of Goshutes asserts sovereign authority over the reservation territory and the activities within it, and claims that the State of Utah has no jurisdiction over this activity. The state claims the responsibility to protect the health and welfare of its citizens. Since the storage of nuclear waste carries risks that persons in counties surrounding the reservation would bear, the state feels obliged to assert its power.

The Goshutes have a right to make this decision through their own government mechanism, and to issue their own guidelines to a waste storage operation that wishes to lease their land. They are obliged neither to consult the State of Utah nor to abide by the regulations of the U.S. Environmental Protection Agency. Just this sort of legal independence makes Indian reservations attractive as potential sites for the treatment or storage of hazardous wastes from the point of view of the companies that operate such facilities. Sometimes companies are willing to pay handsomely for the privilege of working with Indian groups to bypass state and federal regulation. For their part, some Indian groups, such as the Skull Valley Band, find in such leasing arrange-

15. Timothy Egan, "New Prosperity Brings New Conflict to Indian Country," *New York Times*, March 8, 1998, National/Metro sec. As of February 2000, this dispute remains at a standoff. See "Other Nuclear Waste Facilities Being Considered in Utah," *Salt Lake Tribune*, February 20, 2000.

ments a rare opportunity to generate significant income with which they can improve the lives of their members and develop the reservation's infrastructure.

The Goshutes, I have said, do have self-determination rights in this situation. They are a distinct and historically colonized people with a right to preserve their cultural distinctness and enlarge their well-being as a group through their own forms of collective action. On the interpretation of this right of self-determination that I reject, they may simply deny that the State of Utah and the federal government have a right to interfere with their decision. On this interpretation, they can rightfully say that this decision is entirely their business and is none of the business of the State of Utah.

There is no denying, however, that the siting of a nuclear waste storage facility has potential consequences for people living near the reservation. They can be adversely affected if the facility leaks radioactive material into the ground, water, or air. On my account of self-determination, the Goshutes and the citizens of Utah are in a close and ongoing relationship. This relationship, in this case partly defined by geographical proximity, obliges the Goshutes to take the interests of potentially affected citizens of Utah into account.

The apparent approach of the State of Utah to this controversy, however, is to challenge any right to self-determination. The State of Utah apparently would like to have the power to override the Goshute decision, to impose state government power and regulations over this group. It seems that between the two groups we face the alternatives of either recognizing the right of the Indian band to do what it wishes with its territory or recognizing the right of a larger entity around it to exercise final authority over that territory.

More generally, Congress has begun hearings on the question of whether U.S. tribal sovereignty should not be revised or eliminated. There are many in the United States who believe that disputes such as the dispute over nuclear waste are best addressed by eliminating jurisdictional difference. All the people in a contiguous territory, in this case, ought to be subject to the same laws and procedures of decision making. On this account, a state ought to be the overriding, unifying, and final authority, with no independent entities "within" it. When that state is recognized by the international community as a sovereign state, such as the United States or New Zealand, then it has a right of self-determination understood as noninterference. Such a right of noninterference applies particularly to the right of that state to make its own decisions about how it will rule over "its" minorities who claim rights of self-determination in relation to it. All states recognized as independent sovereign states in international law at the moment have such as right of noninterference with respect to "their" indigenous peoples. Hearings considering the question of whether to continue the current system of tribal self-determination assume that the United States has such a right.

From the point of view of indigenous peoples, even those who presently have significant autonomy rights in relation to the states that claim jurisdiction over them, this right of states is illegitimate. The only recourse they have within the logic of national sovereigntists is to assert for themselves the right of autonomy as noninterference. Political standoff, then, is the typical result.

Self-determination understood as relational autonomy, on the other hand, conceives the normative and jurisdictional issues in this dispute as follows. The Skull Valley Band of the Goshutes should be recognized as a self-determining people. This implies that they have self-government rights; through their government they can make decisions about the use of land and resources under their jurisdiction to benefit their members. Thus they may decide to lease land for nuclear waste storage. They do not have an unlimited right of noninterference, however. Communities outside the tribe who claim potential adverse effects to themselves because of tribal decisions have a *claim* upon those activities, and the Goshutes are morally obliged to hear that claim. Intergovernmental relations ought to be so structured such that, when self-governing entities stand in relationships of contiguity or mutual effect, there are settled procedures of discussion and negotiations about conflicts, side effects of their activities, and shared problems. Because parties in a dispute frequently polarize or fail to respect each other, such procedures should include a role for public oversight and arbitration by outside parties with less stake in the dispute. Such procedures of negotiation, however, are very different from being subject to the authority of a state under which more local governments including the indigenous governments stand, and which finally decides the rules.[16]

---

16. Will Kymlicka, *Multicultural Citizenship* (Oxford: Oxford University Press, 1995). Kymlicka argues that national minorities, including indigenous peoples, ought to have recognized self-government rights, and that such rights limit nation-state sovereignty over them without making them separate sovereign states. Kymlicka does not specify the details of the meaning of self-government in a context of negotiated federated relationships as much as one would like, but it is clear that he has something like this in mind.

Final Question: The Rights of Individuals

I have argued that international law ought to continue to recognize a principle of self-determination for peoples and should interpret this principle differently from the traditional principle of noninterference and independence. I have argued for an alternative interpretation of self-determination as relational autonomy in the context of institutions that aim to prevent domination. Some critics worry that claims to self-determination give license to a group to oppress individuals or sub-groups within it. If a people has a right to govern its affairs its own way, these critics object, discriminatory or oppressive practices and policies toward women, particular religious groups, or castes may go unchallenged. This sort of objection has little force, however, if we accept a concept of self-determination conceived as relational autonomy in the context of institutions that minimize domination.

My articulation of a principle of self-determination as nondomination instead of noninterference focused on the relationship between a group and those outside it. If we give priority to a principle of nondomination, however, then it should also apply to the relation between a group and its members. The self-determination of a people should not extend so far as to permit the domination of some of its members by others. For reasons other than those of mutual effects, namely reasons of individual human right, outsiders sometimes have a responsibility to interfere with the self-governing actions of a group in order to prevent severe violations of human rights. This claim introduces a new set of contentious questions, however, about how human rights are defined, who should decide when they have been seriously violated by a government against its members, and the proper agents and procedures of intervention. These important questions are beyond the scope of this essay. A relational concept of self-determination for peoples does not entail that members of the group can do anything they want to other members without interference from those outside. It does entail, however, that insofar as there are global rules defining individual rights and agents to enforce them, all peoples should have the right to be represented *as peoples* in the forums that define and defend those rights. Thus the sort of global regulatory institutions I have said are necessary to prevent domination between peoples should be constituted by the participation of all the peoples regulated by them.

Cultural Choice and the Revision of Freedom

Homi K. Bhabha

Liberals have a way of occupying the high moral ground while keeping the lower depths finely covered, moving convincingly from "causes" to cases, balancing theory and practice. What are the possibilities of maneuver in the midst of such fluency? Susan Okin's "Is Multicultural-ism Bad for Women?" first published in the *Boston Review*, is a case in point.[1] Her central argument is that "there is considerable likelihood of conflict between feminism and group rights for minority cultures, which persists even when the latter are claimed on liberal grounds." This is a useful corrective to the prevailing orthodoxy that establishes "equivalences" between disadvantaged groups, aggregating "commu-nities of interest" without doing the hard work of specifying rights and interests, shying away from conflicts within, and between, minorities.

Let me, however, tweak the sacred cow by its tail (rather than indulging in the phallic fandango of taking the bull by the horn) and suggest that the force of Okin's feminist advocacy rests on a restricted understanding of the "liberal grounds" on which feminism and multi-culturalism *might negotiate* their differences around rights and repre-sentations. Okin's view of the interface between feminism and multi-culturalism is so focused on the conflict generated by the antifeminist and patriarchal effects of criminal cultural defense cases that, against her own best advice, she allows herself to produce "monolithic," though gender-differentiated, characterizations of minority, migrant cultures—kidnap and rape by Hmong men, wife-murder by immi-

---

1. Susan Okin, "Is Multiculturalism Bad for Women?" in *Is Multiculturalism Bad for Women?* ed. Joshua Cohen, Matthew Howard, and Martha C. Nussbaum (Princeton: Princeton University Press, 1999).

grants from Asia and the Middle Eastern countries, mother-child suicide among Japanese and Chinese provoked by the shame of the husband's infidelity.

The cultural defense plea is the ethnographic evidence that
invokes for Okin the "basic idea" that the defendant's cultural group
regards women as subordinates whose primary purpose is to serve
men sexually and domestically. By contrast, Western liberal cultures (a
phrase Okin repeatedly uses to identify which side she is on) discrimi-
nate in practice between the sexes, but the protection of domestic law
produces an enabling and equitable familial culture for girls and
women. Okin's narrative begins by pitting multiculturalism against
feminism but then grows seamlessly into a comparative and evaluative
judgment on minority cultures (largely represented by cultural defense
cases) delivered from the point of view of Western liberal cultures (represented by the eloquent testimony of academic feminists). In my view,
however, issues related to group rights or cultural defense *must* be
placed in the context of the *on*going lives of minorities in the metropol-
itan cultures of the West if we are to understand the deprivation and
discrimination that shape their affective lives, often alienated from the
comforts of citizenship. Minorities are too frequently imaged as the
abject "subjects" of their cultures of origin, huddled in the gazebo of
group rights, preserving the orthodoxy of their distinctive cultures in
the midst of the great storm of Western progress. When this becomes
the dominant opinion within the liberal public sphere—strangely similar to the views held by patriarchal elders within minority communities
whose authority depends upon just such traditionalist essentialisms
and pieties—then minorities are regarded as virtual citizens, never
quite "here and now," relegated to a distanced sense of belonging elsewhere, to a "there and then."

I do not wish to press the tired, overused charge of "Eurocentrism"
against Okin's arguments. Considerably more problematic than the
inappropriate application of "external" norms is the way in which the
truths of Western liberalism become, at once, the measure and mentor
of minority cultures. Western liberalism, warts and all, serves as a sal-
vage operation, if not salvation itself. With a zealousness reminiscent of
the colonial civilizing mission, the "liberal" agenda is articulated without a shadow of self-doubt, except perhaps to acknowledge its contingent failings in the practice of everyday life. If the failures of liberalism

are always "practical," then what kind of perfectibility does the "principle" claim for itself? Okin's choice for "Western liberalism" is not what concerns me here. I am more interested in the fact that what is presented through a kind of cultural casuistry as the conflict between the "group" and the individual (as the bearer of rights) is, in fact, less about the value of particular cultural practices and more about the autonomy of free "choice." As Doriane Coleman neatly sums it up in her survey of U.S. cultural rights cases, "By treating such evidence as exculpatory . . . the message is sent that if you are an immigrant, you are not guaranteed the right *to choose* to escape those aspects of your culture (or those stereotypes of your culture) that collide with the criminal law."[2]

This chapter will explore various aspects of what happens to the ethic and the narrative of "choice" in conditions of cultural diversity or the landscape of cultural difference. What concepts of culture and agency attach to discourses of "choice?" If the "cultural" is an ongoing discursive order or a practice of signification, then does it confuse or conjoin the "singularity" of individuated personhood with a more transindividual or intersubjective sense of enunciation? What is the temporality that signifies the space or place of choice in the narrative of options? Let me write, at the outset, that many of the issues I raise are not local or specific to "multicultural societies" and may have a much more general resonance. That is as it should be for our times. Where I see the specificity of the multicultural is in a certain "symptomatic" strategy where particular general conditions of cultural "undecidability" are identified with cultural diversity. For the sake of economy I have tried to attend "multiculturalism" or "minoritization" as forms of enunciation in a particular relation to their liberal citation; the essential task of specifying subjects of race, gender, class, generation within my more general reflections is a task to follow. At this stage, however, I will only argue that terms like *choice* have an application and a practice of use across discourses of difference, in the context of exercising options that are undoubtedly different in each case.

In the discourse of cultural rights—provoked in large part by the presence of minorities, multiculturalism, immigration, communities of interest—the question of the "right" to a culture turns on the ethical

2. Doriane Coleman, "Individualizing Justice through Multiculturalism: The Liberals' Dilemma," *Columbia Law Review* 96 (June 1996): 1093.

and political freedom of "choice": the freedom to choose a cultural affiliation, the right to be free to constitute or preserve a culture, or indeed
to oppose it by exercising the moral "right of exit." There are of course
many social limitations to cultural choice—poverty, illiteracy, gender,
economic hardship, patriarchalism—but for the moment I want to
examine what is entailed, at the ethical and enunciative level, in this
concept of cultural choosing. For the act of choice also shapes an image
of "selfhood" that plays a normative role in liberal thinking and influ-
ences what it means to be a social agent. But cultural "choice" is not a
one-shot affair, as Will Kymlicka tells us in *Multicultural Citizenship*, his
influential work on cultural rights that has been formative to the discussion on group rights and liberal principles. "[W]hat is distinctive to
the liberal state," he writes, "concerns the forming and revising of people's conception of the good, rather than the pursuit of those conceptions *once chosen*" (my emphasis).[3]

"Choice" and "revision" are part of the continuity of the liberal
individual subject, which differs from the "communitarian" subject
because it can "stand apart," in Kymlicka's phrase, to make a deliberate
choice. The originary, "first" choice has to be supplemented by a second deliberative choice, a kind of "doubling the stakes" of choice, if
you will. Worth noticing here is a peculiar and unacknowledged iterative or supplementary logic—a time lag—related to the enuciative conditions of choice. One could say that liberal "free" cultural choice only
knows its freedom retroactively, once the revisionary choice has been
made. So the freedom attributed to choice, within the liberal discourse,
and the autonomous individual subject that subtends it, is only validated by the fact that a supplementary revisionary choice exists *belatedly after it, endowing it with its autonomy as a kind of delayed action, an
afterwardness.*

This is not simply an argument for saying that choice, by its very
nature, and liberalism by its very culture, require a "plurality" of
options to choose from, *at any one given time* in order, for instance, to
foster pluralism and tolerance. Nor am I suggesting that the first and
second choices are to be sequentially made. They stand in a more conceptual and virtual relationship to each other that resembles in some
ways what Derrida describes as the effect of a double inscription that
produces an *entre*, an in-between, "the effect of a medium . . . located

---

3. Will Kymlicka, *Multicultural Citizenship* (Oxford: Clarendon Press, 1995), 82.

between the two terms . . . an operation that both sows confusion between them and stands between the opposites 'at once.'"[4]

My perverse desire is to dwell on this doubling and displacement of the "temporal" moment of choice that refuses its successive or synchronous embodiment in an individuated moment or a singular subject of choice—at least the second time around. I want to open up, in between the first shot and its revisionary iteration, the question of the *medium* of culture as an ongoing practice of supplementary significa- tion and subject formation/identification, and then to consider its implications for the agency of "choice" in the revisionary, transitional moments of multicultural societies. It is, in particular, the ambivalent and agonistic apparatus of the "cultural" as the location for a double designation of agential choice that interests me: first, culture as a medium that holds "apart" for instance those familiar oppositions—the individual and the group, subject and structure, sign and symbol—but then, those very terms can only be related or represented *through* that "apartness," in between the terms of difference, creating objective cor- relatives from within the significatory "gap." At another remove, cul- ture is envisaged by Joseph Raz and other liberal theorists, less as a *per- formative* medium, and more as a generalizing *precondition* to choice that bestows moral respect and recognition upon the individual as the ethical end-point.

When seen from such "displaced and double" perspectives (cul- ture as performative medium, culture as the precondition for moral autonomy), the familiar opposition between "individual" and "group" that haunts the discourse of cultural rights is no longer polarized or neutralized; *these* polarities exist, as we shall see, in a temporal and enunciative movement, a vacillation of "ends" that Raz describes for "value pluralism" as having "no single balance . . . one is forever mov- ing from one to the other from time to time."[5] The effect of such a "dou- ble balance," if I may turn Raz's phrase, is not to display some endless derring-do of "dis-closure." It puts me largely in agreement with Eti- enne Balibar, who suggests that "while rights are always attributed to individuals, in the last instance, they are achieved and won collectively. . . . Man is identified not with a *given* or an essence, be it natural or

---

4. Jacques Derrida, *Dissemination*, trans. Barbara Johnson (Chicago: University of Chicago Press, 1981), 212.

5. Joseph Raz, "Multiculturalism: A Liberal Perspective," in *Ethics in the Public Domain* (Oxford: Clarendon Press, 1994), 165.

supra-natural, but with a practice and a task [what I have identified as the ongoing, nonsynchronous performance of cultural difference]. This idea actually combines . . . an ontological proposition: the property of the human being is the collective or the transindividual construction of his individual autonomy; and . . . an ethical proposition: the value of human agency arises from the fact that no one can be liberated by others, although no one can liberate herself or himself *without others*."[6]

If the revision of ends affirms the liberty of the individual, it also generates an ethical narrative that frequently subjects the individual to a national or nationalized prerogative of cultural belonging. Kymlicka argues, for instance, that a national identity is crucial for a liberal culture because the revision of ends "is not primarily the freedom to go beyond one's language and history, but rather the freedom to move around within one's societal culture."[7] The ethicality of the good life yields somewhat too easily, for my taste, to the nation-bound morality of the good citizen.

What then of cultural choice, of the revision of ends, in the transnational contexts of migration, in the conditions of multicultural translation, where societies are passing through, to cite Walter Benjamin, the "continua of transformation, not abstract areas of identity and similarity"?[8] What do cultural options look like from the optics of exile or migration?

> What does it mean to be a good immigrant? . . . [I]s the good immigrant the one who shares his material success with his comrades at home, or the one who invests in her new country? . . . Is the good immigrant the one who brings up assimilated children, or the one who preserves a bit of the culture of his homeland? Does being a good immigrant imply obeying the laws of the host country? And, do the laws to be obeyed include the immigration laws?[9]

Teresa Sullivan asks these questions in a special issue of the *International Migration Review* on the ethics of migration. She suggests that

---

6. Étienne Balibar, "Subjection and Subjectivation," in *Supposing the Subject*, ed. Joan Copjec (New York: Verso, 1994), 12.

7. Kymlicka, *Multicultural Citizenship*, 90.

8. Walter Benjamin, "On Language as Such and on the Language of Man," in *Selected Writings*, vol. 1, *1913–1926*, ed. Marcus Bullock and Michael W. Jennings (Cambridge, Mass.: Belknap Press, 1996), 70.

9. Teresa Sullivan, "Immigration and the Ethics of Choice," *International Migration Review* 30 (spring 1996): 98.

there are no clear answers or guidelines because the "social role of immigrant does not carry with it a lot of normative expectations." It is a feature of *multicultural* societies that there is, around the issue of cultural choice, an intensification of a normative underspecificity or indeterminacy. (At the judicial level there is often a similar problem of cultural underspecification and racial overinterpretation in constructing "fictive identities" in double-jeopardy deportation cases, for example against long-settled North African migrants in France.) In a vein similar to Sullivan's argument, Rainer Baubock extends Charles Taylor's notion of the politics of recognition to suggest that "seeing cultures also as objects of choice includes the additional options of multiple membership and toleration of syncretic and hybrid practices."[10] More significant than the diversity of objects are the disjunct temporalities—successive, cumulative, or continuous—that constitute cultural codes that inform cultural practices and provide the grounds for choice.

In proposing a dialogical notion of toleration, Bhiku Parekh emphasizes the growing gap in multicultural societies between "the so-called core or fundamental values" and "the structured relations of organized public life,"[11] such that the public sphere increasingly becomes an intermediate realm of civic relations consisting of operative public values. They constitute an interstitial *medium* of choice that sows confusion between core values and structured realities, while standing between them, *at the same time,* as the contingent realm of operative practices (Balibar). Under the pressure of multicultural choice, civic relationality becomes a partial and metonymic form of social knowledge that is

> interlocked in the sense that each [operational value] limits and [only] partly defines the contents of the others. They are embodied in institutions and practices that cannot be neatly catalogued or summarized. They are of varying degrees of generality, interpenetrate each other, and cannot be easily individuated. By and large they form a complex whole from which none can be abstracted without distortion.[12]

---

10. Rainer Baubock, "Cultural Minority Rights for Immigrants," *International Migration Review* 30 (spring 1996): 209.

11. Bhiku Parekh, "Minority Practices and Principles of Toleration," *International Migration Review* 30 (spring 1996): 260–61.

12. Ibid., 261.

Multicultural civic relations, in Parekh's account, constitute bodies of knowledge and "subjects of culture" that have an estranged relation to *themselves;* their values cannot be individuated, cataloged, or summarized, and although they resist a holistic or homogeneous form of cultural mediation or identification, any exclusion or abstraction of an element from the lifeworld of civic relations—that in-between area— will paradoxically distort and deform the "whole." What, we may ask, can the epistemological or ethical aspects of this "wholeness" be, caught as it is in an *unindividuated* relay or replay between core and structure?

An eloquent answer, made in the spirit of cultural value as a category of displacement and estrangement in the multicultural world, comes by way of Clifford Geertz's Tanner lecture, entitled, "The Uses of Diversity."[13] Geertz tries to transform the traditional concept of culture-as-self-containedness with the estranging, ethical responsibility of encountering "diversity" and thus engaging with a "strangeness" or alterity at the moment of *its* enunciation "to refocus our attention . . . [and] make us visible to ourselves," Geertz writes, "by representing us and everyone else as cast into the midst of a world full of irremovable strangenesses we can't keep clear of."[14] The location of this strangeness is not the binary or polar difference between cultures; it is not, Geertz assures us, "the distant tribe, enfolded upon itself in coherent difference,"[15] but a disjunctive, anxious terrain of "sudden faults and dangerous passages"[16] that produces moral asymmetries within the boundary of a *we* such that strangenesses are more oblique and shaded, less easily set off as anomalies "scrambled together in ill-defined expanses, social spaces whose edges are unfixed, irregular, and difficult to locate."[17] And then, that splendid summation: "Foreignness does not start at the water's edge but at the skin's."[18]

Too true, I would say. But, it is the *amniotic* structure of cultural spacing—a watery skin if ever there was one—a "difference" that is at once liminal and fluid, that Geertz cannot fully grasp as the *temporal movement that crosses between* the boundaries of cultural containment.

---

13. Clifford Geertz, "The Uses of Diversity and the Future of Ethnocentrism," *Michigan Quarterly Review* 25 (winter 1985): 105–23.
    14. Ibid., 120.
    15. Ibid., 117.
    16. Ibid., 119.
    17. Ibid., 121.
    18. Ibid., 112.

The moral dilemmas arising from the communication and coexistence of cultural diversity are, within his argument, insistently represented in *spatial metaphors* that set the ground for "puzzles of judgment." Ill-defined expanses, social spaces whose edges are unlocatable, uneven terrains, dangerous passages, clefts and contours are offered as the ethnographic conditions of a new cultural episteme. Geertz spatializes the contingent, incomplete temporalities of ethical-political practice, into a landscape of juxtaposed terrains of knowledge that install him in the Archimedean position, meditating on the fact that "the world is coming at each of its local points to look more like a Kuwaiti bazaar than like an English gentleman's club (to instance what, to my mind— perhaps because I have never been in either of them—are the polar cases)."[19]

It is Raz's belief that such situations of "subcultural anomie" cannot be adequately assuaged by revising toleration within civic relations (Parekh) or applying the remedy of "nondiscrimination rights" to the moral asymmetries within the boundary of a "we" (Geertz). This leads him to propose what he calls "multiculturalism without territorial separation."[20] If Kymlicka suggested that liberal choice was not a "one-shot deal," leading me to open up the cultural as an interstitial, time-lagged space of operation—theoretical and social—then for Raz's theory of "value pluralism," social practices do not constitute successive or cumulative options "as if they come one by one."[21] Echoing Geertz's topography of a "world of irremovable strangenesses," Raz's terrain of multicultural ethical choice is articulated through "the core options which give meaning to our lives," constructed within "dense webs of complex actions and interactions, . . . the density of their details defy[ing] explicit learning or comprehensive articulation."[22] The temporality of such cultural representation is neither synchronous nor successive: social practices are "conglomerations of interlocking practices which constitute the range of life options."[23] To effect a choice in this context, Raz continues, makes it impossible for the subject or the individual "to consider and decide deliberately. . . . [A] lot has to be done, so to speak automatically. But to fit into a pattern, that automatic aspect

---

19. Ibid., 121.
20. Raz, "Multiculturalism," 159.
21. Ibid., 162.
22. Ibid.
23. Ibid.

of behaviour [call it ideology, interpellation, subjectification, discourse] has to be guided, to be directed and channeled into a coherent meaningful whole."[24]

If the deliberative rational individual is now also a subject interpellated "automatically" by interlocking practices, then it is not simply "density" or diversity that baffles choice; rather, the subject is designated as "decentered" and "displaced" at the point of evaluating options and making choices. What Raz describes as "automatic behavior" is close to what Judith Butler sees as the citationality of "excitable speech" in multicultural contexts: "Indeed," Butler writes, "is iterability or citationality not precisely this: *the operation of that metalepsis by which the subject who 'cites' the performative is temporarily produced as the belated and fictive origin of the performative itself?*"[25] We now have the spectacle of the attenuation of the free liberal subject: not unfree because of the restrictions on choice or the plurality of choice as "objects," but "dependent," since the individual is a mediated subject of enunciation, caught in the performative, contingent logic of cultural "representation," in the very enactment of the discourse of multicultural "value plurality."

At this point of utterance, the "autonomic" individual subject becomes uncannily confronted with its agonistic double. What occurs within the body of Raz's discussion of value pluralism is a kind of discursive or enunciative split, a double inscription in relation to choice. One form of the conflict of choice, Raz argues, is endemic to value pluralism and is consensual in nature. It maintains *the moral mastery* and the autonomy of the self and conforms to the mundane reality that "two values are incompatible if they cannot be realized or pursued to the fullest degree in a single life. . . . What one loses is of a different kind from what one gains. . . . [F]aced with valuable options . . . one simply [chooses] one way of life rather than another, both being good and not susceptible to comparison of degree."[26] But "affirmative multiculturalism" can bring no such closure and composure to the subject of cultural choice. Its subjectivity is perfomatively constituted in the very tension that makes knowledges of cultural difference dense, conglomerative, and nondeliberative; its mastery of its own choice is unsettled by what

---

24. Ibid., 161–62.
25. Judith Butler, *Excitable Speech: A Politics of the Performative* (New York: Routledge, 1997), 49.
26. Raz, "Multiculturalism," 164.

Raz describes as the automatic aspect of behavior that continually raises the challenge of the *contingent* to the claim for coherence, the desire to achieve a "meaningful whole" in the narrative of a life or a society. This is the agonistic and ambivalent subject of a double, decentered multicultural choice:

> Tension is an inevitable concomitant of accepting the truth of value-pluralism [in the context of affirmative multiculturalism]. And it is a tension without stability, without a definite resting point of reconciliation of the two perspectives, the one recognizing the validity of competing values and the one hostile to them. There is no point of equilibrium, no single balance which is correct and could prevail to bring the two perspectives together. One is forever moving from one to the other from time to time.[27]

Raz tries to rescue this aporetic, split choice of "difference" or cultural incommensurability that vacillates, moving from one to the other, struggling between cultural norms, between interpellation and agency, the automatic and the autonomic. He attempts to reinstate the individualist subject through the moral rhetoric of "respect"; but respect finally becomes a way of "standing back or apart" from the most radical proposal of "value pluralism," that is, to place the subject of ethical and political choice at that point of "no equilibrium," no single balance. And then, "in the moving from one to the other," he seeks to reconfigure the contest of choice and the "subject" of culture. Respect struggles to still the movement of the iterative, double temporality—in Raz's phrase, the movement "from time to time to time"—that haunts the tension and anxiety, the ambivalence and agonism, that constitutes the revision of ends, which to inscribe an agent, also requires there to be a revision in the narrative of ethical "means."

My emphasis on the double and displaced nature of cultural "choice" attempts to unsettle the validation of the autonomic subject, as well as the divisions and distances through which it maintains its "apodictic" authority in matters of cultural judgment and identification. It is a certainty based not on denying cultural diversity as *content*—which liberalism celebrates—but in reproducing, each time, the same place or position of judgment in a structure of the subject: forever *standing apart*.

---

27. Ibid., 165.

To reconstitute the question of choice, to relearn the language of freedom, requires that we not merely rethink the ends of freedom, but
focus on the middle, the *entre*, culture as a medium of betweenness. The
shift I am suggesting through the structure of "double-and-displaced"
choice is a narrative of the subject, discursive or practical, that occupies
the space in between "instantiating" choice and its iterative, revisionary double. Parekh occupies such a space in the in-between, unspecifi-
able realm of the civic relation; Geertz in the asymmetries of cultures-
in-between and betwixt; and Raz, in the tension and the torsion of
value pluralism and its sense of loss.

What is the relation of the cultural subject to agency in such discursive and enunciatory conditions? The subject is not what you start
with, as an origin, nor where you end, as closure. The subject is what is
discovered about the movement of discourse, texts, action without
those polarities. The subject is a strategy of authorization and differen-
tiation that produces an anteriority before the beginning, and a futurity
beyond the end, where the present is the time of decision and choice, at
once deliberate and disjunctive, at once survival and sovereignty. Or to
put it in Hannah Arendt's words: "Most action and speech is concerned
with this in-between . . . which for all its intangibility is no less real than
the world of things we visibly have in common. . . . Although everybody started his life by inserting himself into the human world through
action and speech, nobody is the author or producer of his own life-
story. In other words, the stories, the results of action and speech reveal
an agent, but this agent is not an author or producer. Somebody began
it and is its subject in the twofold sense of the word, namely actor and
sufferer, but nobody is its author."[28] For this twofold sense of choice,
both originary and revisionary, actor and sufferer, and made from the
in-between, there is no standing apart at the moment of judgment.

I am not in any position to take what I am proposing as a shift in
the subject of cultural choice and turn it into a full-scale theory of rights.
What I am attempting to do, in a very tentative way, is to make an intervention by activating a certain ambivalence that exists within the discourse of autonomic choice and freedom. For instance, Patricia
Williams argues for a theory of rights on the grounds of respect for
minorities, because they are then placed "in the referential range of self
and others, that elevates one's status from human body to social

28. Hannah Arendt, *The Human Condition* (Chicago: University of Chicago Press,
1958), 182–84.

being."[29] But she does this, please note, after citing the "thick" description of "need" and survival that has been part of the descriptive literary experience of Afro-Americans, her own writing no less. Without that literary discourse of need that places the subject in that kind of enunciative space I have described—subject without order, doubleness of choice—constituted in the circulation of contingency of meanings and significances, Williams would end up where she would not want to be: arguing for rights that are based on the individual. As it is, she violates the "individualist" approach by arguing, with literary jeu d'esprit, that rights should be given away profligately to "collective goods" where no autonomic subject lurks: "Unlock them from reification by giving them to slaves. Give them to trees. Give them to cows. Give them to history."[30] And that is of course to say that you cannot give them to a "subject" that is not seen as part of the mediatory narratives of culture as a performative ongoing relational act that is not invested in autonomy as it is in a kind of performativity that moves in an interstitial space between groupishness and individuation, between having and doing, exactly the space of culture as a mediatory and significatory activity.

"Why are the bonds of language and culture so strong for most people?" To answer this question Kymlicka refers us to the political and legal philosophical work of Raz and Avishai Margalit. Margalit's response to the question about *national* belonging through the "bonds of language and culture" returns us to my starting point about the "double" and displaced structure of liberal "choice"—at once initiatory and supplementary, a kind of future anteriority or *après coup*. It also allows me to take further my contention that the "stand apart" autonomic subject, and its identificatory axes—individual or group—is inadequate to deal with ethical revisionary choice as a culturally and discursively mediated effect. What provides a societal culture with its shared vocabulary and its communal solidarity is, according to Margalit, "respect for humans." The particular cultural trait that "justifies" such respect is the capacity for cultural freedom, "the capacity . . . of reevaluating one's life at any given moment, as well as the ability to change one's life from this moment on."[31] Here, once again we have the

---

29. Patricia Williams, *The Alchemy of Race and Rights* (Cambridge: Harvard University Press, 1991), 153.
30. Ibid., 165.
31. Avishai Margalit, *The Decent Society*, trans. Naomi Goldblum (Cambridge: Harvard University Press, 1996), 70.

justificatory "revisionary" choice—the choice that establishes the right
to culture and a culture of rights—but with a difference. The condition
of freedom, Margalit acknowledges, must derive its agency and its ethical direction from a discontinuity, a disjunction between "first choice"
and "revisionary ends." "Every person," Margalit argues, "is capable
of a future way of life that is *discontinuous* with the past. The respect
people deserve for this is based precisely on the fact that Man does not
have a nature."[32] The following extended metaphor moves between a
theory of language and the meaning of life; in it, Margalit gives a hint
of the basis on which we may need to rethink both the "subject" of
choice and the enunciation of freedom:

> There is a deep analogy between the concept of linguistic meaning
> and the concept of the meaning of life. Linguistic meaning accords
> with the possibility that the series of uses a term has had in the past
> does not determine its uses in the future. Linguistic uses are not
> railroad tracks set up in advance, so that the only thing to worry
> about is the possibility of the engine going off the track. The same
> is true of the meaning of life: not only do the totality of all one's
> past actions fail to determine the path of one's future actions, but
> even the interpretation one has given to one's past actions can be
> reevaluated at any given moment.[33]

How can we understand such contingency and discontinuity as defining the moment of the reflection on, and revision of, cultural "choice?"
Can contingency and arbitrariness such as the signifier entails be part
of a cultural narrative that shapes the "agency" of culture as a practice
of freedom? Where is the space—or indeed, the time—to *stand back* at
the point of revision?

   I have now skirted so dangerously close to issues I have recently
raised in a reading of Adrienne Rich that I cannot resist her siren song.

> Old backswitching road bent toward the ocean's light
> Talking of angles of vision   movements   a black or a red tulip
>   opening
> Times of walking across a street   thinking
> not *I have joined a movement* but   *I am stepping in this deep current*

---

32. Ibid., 71; emphasis added.
33. Ibid.

Part of my life washing behind me   terror I couldn't swim with
part of my life waiting for me   a part I had no words for
I need to live each day through   have them and know them all
though I can see from here where I'll be standing at the end.

———————

When does a life bend toward freedom? grasp its direction?
How do you know you're not circling in pale dreams, nostalgia,
        stagnation
but entering that deep current   malachite, colorado
requiring all your strength wherever found
your patience and your labor
desire pitted against desire's inversion
all your mind's fortitude?
Maybe through a teacher: someone with facts with numbers
        with poetry
who wrote on the board: IN EVERY GENERATION ACTION FREES
        OUR DREAMS.
Maybe a student: one mind unfurling like a redblack peony
·   ·   ·   ·   ·   ·   ·   ·   ·   ·   ·   ·   ·   ·   ·   ·   ·   ·
—And now she turns her face brightly on the new morning in
        the new classroom
new in her beauty her skin her lashes her lively body:
Race, class . . . all that . . . but isn't all that just history?
Aren't people bored with it all?

She could be
myself at nineteen   but free of reverence for past ideas
ignorant of hopes piled on her   She's a mermaid
momentarily precipitated from a solution
which could stop her heart   She could swim or sink
like a beautiful crystal.[34]

Written from the in-between, the doubling and displacement of
choice that I have described, the poem's revisionary project produces a
disjunction in the subject's encounter with itself. The moment of its
emergence as a "group" subject is also the moment of its consciousness
of its own "belatedness"; in between the subject's past ("part of my life

———————

34. Adrienne Rich, "Two: movement," from "Inscriptions," in *Dark Fields of the
Republic: Poems, 1991–1995* (New York: W. W. Norton, 1995), 61–62.

washing behind me") and its "anachronous," yet inexorable, future ("part of my life waiting for me a part I had no words for"), lies the shifting present. This subtle process of negotiation between "persons" that inhabit the "same" subject (differently), and differential temporalities that constitute the "same" historical event (disjunctively), reveals the complex scenario of politics as a transformational process. By emphasizing politics as *movement* Rich turns it into a negotiated *(un)settlement* (if I might coin a term) between the agential first person—*I*—confronted by the anachronous proximity of its split double—*you*—that is future's part, the revisionary "person to come."

It is the space and time of the "present," signified in the poem not as an idea or concept, but as a kind of *verbal act or action of articulation,* that occupies this "gap" in time and knowledge. The unfulfilled or "unsatisfied" present becomes the site of a certain futurity, of freedom as a *project* (in both senses of the word) that has to be negotiated. Or, as Sartre explains ec-static freedom, "the given, choice, the situation, goal. . . . [T]his totalisation is impossible because there is no homogeneity of elements. . . . And if the dialectic is not a closed system, then we have to live with the incertitude of the present moment . . . [while] the future dimension is risk, uncertainty, a wager."[35] Taking part in a "revision of ends" as a form of collective *recognition* becomes also a process of "being" taken apart at the level of identification.

Margalit's linguistic map of the difficult world of "respect" and the capacity to "respect" revision stands at the end of a certain liberal tradition, while Rich's colorado of conflict and incommensurable selfhood initiates the agonistic socialist politics of the new social movements. For Margalit there is a need to partially underscore the "autonomic" subject, to disturb the poise of its "standing apart," by introducing "discontinuity" on the wings of the "floating," arbitrary signifier. However, fearing that, Icarus-like, the wax wings may melt, Margalit normalizes the contingent moment of "revision" that he initially proposes through the "radical freedom"[36] of the sign, by introducing the device of *homines ex machina,* not quite standing apart, a little laid low perhaps, but holding on to an attenuated autonomy: "The engine of life can change direction at the will of the driver, even if some directions are easier to travel in than others."[37] For Margalit the ethical source of

---

35. Jean Paul Sartre, *Notebooks for an Ethics,* trans. David Pellauer (Chicago: University of Chicago Press, 1992), 464, 467.

36. Margalit, *The Decent Society,* 71.

37. Ibid.

respect is a temporal category—"the future must remain open"—but in exploding its continuity with the past, he leaves the present oddly untouched, strangely secure. What of the "present" in which the choice of revision must take place? I shall not labor the point that Adrienne Rich has made so poignantly and pointedly about the "discontinuity" of the present, and the ec-static ethics of a revision of ends, that leaves you standing in a midstness, in the metonymic movement of the unfinished present, missing the conjunctive loci of your life. What I want to do is to push Margalit's argument beyond his initial claim of respect for the capacity of discontinuity in the act of revision—as a basic human value—to advance it toward the problem of the ethics and politics of the "recognition" of cultural or minority difference in what he terms a decent society. I am, of course, moving him from his notion of an "open future" to confront a kind of "presentness," a quotidian quality, a more fallen moment.

In his chapter entitled "Culture"—a category that he claims is semiotic, "an extension of the concept of language to cover systems of signs and symbols in general"[38]—Margalit does engage a politics of the present. The present happens when the semiosis of culture turns "active" and performative, like the everyday "tics" of our thinking. This cannot be seen simply as the "problem of ideology" without risking another instrumental or "symptomatic" argument. In the moment of revisionary choice there is no "standing back" of the subject (even if, like Althusser, you take your stand in the Lacanian Imaginary), for we are in a world of "collective representations" that are at once the medium and agent of choice. There is a partial fulfillment of my own earlier claim that the agency of "revisionary" cultural choice requires an enunciation that cannot be consigned to the binary disposition of choice as a group right *versus* an individual right. The mode of "choice" as a doubled and displaced agency that I have suggested through my readings of Kymlicka, Raz, and Rich, echoes productively with Foucault's description of the *practice* of language and culture, calculated at the point of the agency of meaning, the agony of choice:

> A statement is not confronted (face to face, as it were) by a corre-
> late—or the absence of a correlate [no standing apart]. . . . The ref-
> erential of the statement forms the place, the condition, the field of
> emergence, the authority to differentiate between individuals or

---

38. Ibid., 166.

objects, states of things and relations that are brought into play by the statement itself. . . . It is this *group* [or groupishness] that characterizes the enunciative level of the formulation.[39]

As we gather in the terrain of our times, where the "face to face" is veiled by distance or difference, and any desire for "transparency" is trammeled in the continua of translation or transformation, we are often left in the place of the questioner: what kind of "subjects" would we have to be to participate in the "revision of ends and means" without "standing apart"; what does it require to be at once inside and outside the encompassing group; how can we survive caught as we are, unbalanced or recovering our posture, somewhere between "self-respect and the criticism of the other?"

---

39. Michel Foucault, *The Archaeology of Knowledge and the Discourse on Language* (New York: Pantheon Books, 1972), 91.

Durkheim Revisited: Human Rights as the Moral Discourse for the Postcolonial, Post–Cold War World

Jane F. Collier

At the end of the last century, Durkheim advocated something very close to human rights as the appropriate moral discourse for a modern society with a well-developed division of labor.[1] Growing up in the aftermath of the failed social revolutions of 1848, at a time that historian Eric Hobsbawm has characterized as the "Age of Capital,"[2] Durkheim wanted to find a moral discourse that avoided laissez-faire capitalism's apparent celebration of amoral self-interest without reinscribing the religious moralities of the past or succumbing to Communist class warfare. One hundred years later, when neoliberal economic policies are once again spreading around the globe in the aftermath of Communism's apparent failure, the moral discourse of human rights is being widely advocated by people who, like Durkheim, fear capitalism's privileging of profits over people, the possibility of class warfare, and

---

I would like to thank Saba Mahmood, Austin Sarat, Sally Merry, and George Collier for their helpful suggestions on earlier drafts of this essay. Research in Zinacantán was supported by the National Science Foundation, Grant SBR-97–10396, "Mapping Inter-legality in Chiapas, Mexico."

1. Emile Durkheim, *The Division of Labor in Society*, trans. George Simpson (Glencoe, Ill.: Free Press of Glencoe, 1933). Subsequent references will be given in the text.

2. Eric Hobsbawm, *The Age of Capital, 1848–1875* (London: Weidenfeld and Nicolson, 1975).

efforts by "extremist" religious groups to co-opt state power for enforc-
ing their own visions of God's laws.

Human rights today are most commonly identified with such civil
and political rights as the right not to be tortured, subjected to arbitrary
arrest, or denied a fair trial by the government of one's state. But the
modern discourse of human rights includes far more than individual
freedom from state persecution. The 1948 Universal Declaration of
Human Rights (UDHR) actually articulates a broad moral vision of the
just society. In addition to political rights, it lists such economic rights
as the "right to work" and the "right to rest and leisure," such social
rights as the "right to a standard of living" adequate for health and
well-being, and such cultural rights as the "right freely to participate in
the cultural life of the community." As stated in its preamble, the
UDHR was intended to herald "the advent of a world in which human
beings shall enjoy freedom of speech and belief and freedom from fear
and want." It is this broad moral vision of people free from fear and
want, as well as free to speak their minds, that coincides with
Durkheim's vision of the appropriate moral order for modern society.

In this essay, I will explore Durkheim's insight that human rights
is the appropriate moral discourse for modern capitalist society.
Instead of joining debates over whether human rights can be advanced
without thwarting efforts to develop indigenous legal traditions or
whether there are ways of talking about human rights that can avoid
the twin dangers of universalism and cultural relativism, I want to
argue that we need to assess the capacity of human rights discourses to
ameliorate the harmful effects of capitalist market relationships.[3]
Durkheim was right that capitalism and human rights go together.
Whether we like it or not, the spread of capitalist market relations
around the world is being accompanied by the spread of human rights
discourses.[4] As a result, we need to explore the economic and political
contexts that shape whether and how appeals to human rights can help
those most harmed by capitalism's impact.

---

3. I follow such authors as Pheng Cheah, "Posit(ion)ing Human Rights in the Current Global Conjuncture," *Public Culture* 9 (1997): 233, and Kirstie M. McClure, "Taking
Liberties in Foucault's Triangle: Sovereignty, Discipline, Governmentality, and the Subject
of Rights," in *Identities, Politics and Rights,* ed. Austin Sarat and Thomas R. Kearns (Ann
Arbor: University of Michigan Press, 1995), 149, in suggesting that we need to assess the
capacity of human rights discourses to ameliorate the harmful effects of capitalism.

4. Richard A. Wilson, "Human Rights, Culture, and Context: An Introduction," in
Human Rights, Culture, and Context: Anthropological Perspectives, ed. Richard A. Wilson
(London: Pluto Press, 1997), 10.

Durkheim posited an inherent link between economy and morality when he attributed the social problems of his day to the fact that morality had not yet caught up with the increasing division of labor. Because he believed that humans develop their understanding of themselves and the world through interacting with others, he argued that men (and Durkheim did mean males) who performed different tasks would develop different understandings. A high division of labor promoted individualism by stimulating each man to develop his own talents and ideas.[5] Durkheim approved of the division of labor. He was an evolutionist who celebrated both the advances of modern technology and the individuality he believed went with them. Problems arose, however, because men's lack of shared experiences could lead them to lose sight of how each individual contributed to the social whole. Men who felt isolated from others could experience anomie, leading some to commit suicide. And men who failed to recognize the contributions of others could selfishly disregard their needs and humanity. For example, capitalists who attributed profits solely to their own efforts might ruthlessly exploit workers by driving wages below subsistence levels, or alienated workers might advocate class warfare to kill off greedy capitalists. The solution to these problems of anomie and selfish disregard for the well-being of others, Durkheim argued, was not to be found in returning to the religious moralities of the past. Rather, industrial society needed to develop a moral system appropriate to its own needs.

Durkheim argued against returning to the religious moralities of the past in part because he believed that such a return was impossible. The division of labor, which fostered individuality, destroyed the collective experience that, in Durkheim's view, was the foundation of religious sentiment. Moreover, the division of labor tended to produce its own form of religion: "As all the other beliefs and all the other practices take on a character less and less religious, the individual becomes the object of a sort of religion. We erect a cult in behalf of personal dignity which, as every strong cult, already has its superstitions" (172). This "cult of the individual," however, could not form the basis of a modern moral order. Although it, like previous religions, is "common in so far as the community partakes of it" and "turns all wills towards the same end," the common end toward which all wills are turned is individual

---

5. Durkheim believed that only men would develop individual personalities because only their labor would become differentiated with an increase in the division of labor. Durkheim expected women's brains to shrink as the increasing division of labor confined women more and more to the home and repetitive domestic tasks.

self-realization rather than communal solidarity. Durkheim, in fact, accused those who made the cult of the individual "basic in their moral doctrine"—such as laissez-faire capitalists—of fomenting the "dissolution of society" (172).

Having concluded that "all social links which result from likeness progressively slacken" with the increasing division of labor, Durkheim argued that social cohesion needs to be sought elsewhere: "Since mechanical solidarity [based on common experiences] progressively becomes enfeebled, life properly social must decrease or another solidarity must slowly come in to take the place of that which has gone" (173). Durkheim found this new social solidarity in the division of labor itself, which linked "men" through their shared need for one another rather than through their sharing of common experiences: "It is the division of labor which, more and more, fills the role that was formerly filled by the common conscience. It is the principal bond of social aggregates of higher types" (173).

A high division of labor, however, could produce social solidarity "only if it is spontaneous and in proportion as it is spontaneous. But by spontaneity we must understand not simply the absence of all express violence, but also of everything that can even indirectly shackle the free unfolding of the social force that each carries in himself" (377). This is a crucial caveat, and it is the point at which Durkheim lays out his ideas about the kind of moral system needed by modern society.

Durkheim assigned the task of promoting spontaneity to the legal system. He argued against laissez-faire economists who located liberty in the absence of government regulations. Such an absence, Durkheim argued, would not only promote anomie but undermine liberty as well, because "liberty itself is the product of regulation" (386). In order to promote liberty, however, government regulations must be of a particular kind. They must enforce the equality of opportunity needed to ensure that people experience their contractual relations as based on consent rather than force: "If contracts were observed only by force or through fear of force, contractual solidarity would be very precarious. A wholly external order would badly cover disturbances too general to be indefinitely controlled" (382).[6] Durkheim thus concluded,

---

6. Because Durkheim defined a contract as "fully consented to only if the services exchanged have an equivalent social value," he concluded that "it is necessary that the contracting parties be placed in conditions externally equal" (*Division of Labor*, 383).

The task of the most advanced societies is, then, a work of justice.
. . . Just as the ideal of lower societies was to create or maintain as
intense a common life as possible, in which the individual was
absorbed, so our ideal is to make social relations always more equitable, so as to assure the free development of all our socially useful
forces. (387).

Durkheim's ideal of justice as equality of opportunity is enshrined
in human rights documents written more than half a century after he
articulated the "task of the most advanced societies." Even though the
most common understanding of human rights today is as freedom
from state persecution, echoing Durkheim's vision that there must be
"an absence of all express violence," the documents also articulate
Durkheim's vision that governments should undertake the task of
making "social relations always more equitable." The economic, social,
and cultural rights articulated in human rights documents echo
Durkheim's vision that individuals must be free from fear and want—
as well as free from government persecution—if they are to experience
their contractual relations as based on consent rather than force.

Because Durkheim was uncannily right in predicting the evolution
of human rights documents in advanced societies, his analysis is worth
taking seriously. Even if one might prefer an ethical system based on
the obligation to care for others rather than on the protection of individual rights, the fact remains that "rights talk" carries far more power
than "care talk" in the world today. It is not an accident that the Universal Declaration of Human Rights is not a declaration of human
responsibilities. It is also true that rights talk is spreading rapidly, as
more and more groups whose economic systems were once marginal to
capitalism are participating in capitalist market relations. It is therefore
important to consider where Durkheim was right, and where he went
wrong, if we are to explore how—and whether—those suffering from
capitalism's impact might use the discourse of human rights to
improve their situations.

Durkheim seems to have been right when he identified justice in
the modern world as the "equitable social relations" that would enable
individuals to give their free consent to contracts. This vision of justice
has long been associated with capitalism. When land was first being
enclosed and privatized, moralists argued that those who would be
deprived of access to land by privatization needed to be given other

resources so that they could maintain their independence by providing for their basic needs with their own labor. Thomas Paine, for example, in a pamphlet titled *Agrarian Justice* written in 1795–96, argued that "all those who have been thrown out of their natural inheritance by the introduction of a system of landed property" should, by right not charity, be given a sum of money from a national fund to start their own businesses.[7] And the English author of the 1808 *General Report on Enclosures* argued that the poor "should be enabled to supply their necessities, and derive their comforts, through the means of their own industry." This solution, however, required laws to ensure that jobs paid fair wages: "I contend . . . that an equitable balance should be restored between the earnings of an industrious, sober, and willing labourer, and the cost of house rent, and the necessary articles of sustenance and clothing for himself, and a family of average numbers."[8] Or, in the words of the UDHR, written a century and a half later: "Everyone who works has the right to just and favorable remuneration ensuring for himself and his family an existence worthy of human dignity" (Article 23).

Durkheim was also right, I think, to identify selfish disregard for the well-being of others as an important problem, if not the most important problem, of modern capitalist society. Although Durkheim condemned both the laissez-faire capitalists and the communists of his day for this sin, he directed more of his attention at countering the arguments of laissez-faire capitalists than those of communists. Communists who advocated slaughtering capitalist oppressors might be as guilty of failing to recognize the humanity of their opponents as greedy capitalists who pushed wages below subsistence levels, but capitalists were the ones who needed to change if Durkheim's vision of justice was to prevail. Regulations had to ensure that capitalists provided jobs that paid living wages.[9]

When Durkheim condemned the selfishness of modern society, he did not extend his analysis to the family. Like the author of the report on enclosures and the authors of the UDHR, Durkheim apparently

---

7. Thomas Paine, "Agrarian Justice," in *Pioneers of Land Reform,* ed. M. Beer (London: G. Bell and Sons, 1920), 185–187.

8. Arthur Young, *General Report on Enclosures* (New York: Augustus Kelley, 1971).

9. Durkheim also advocated regulations inhibiting the "hereditary transmission of wealth." He argued that inherited wealth "is enough to make the external conditions under which the conflict [the struggle for existence] takes place very unequal, for it gives advantages to some which are not necessarily in keeping with their personal worth" (*Division of Labor,* 378).

assumed that male wage earners would use their wages to feed, clothe, and house their wives and children. Yet the increasing feminization of poverty, which is also the poverty of children and elderly people without capital or adequate pensions, suggests that the problem of selfishness runs deeper than Durkheim or those other writers imagined. Durkheim's understanding that the cult of the individual promotes the dissolution of society needs to be extended to recognize that it also promotes the dissolution of the family.

Durkheim attributed the rampant selfishness he observed to the increasing technological division of labor that isolated workers from one another and so made it difficult for them to appreciate everyone's contribution to the social whole. But I am more convinced by Marx's argument that it is capitalism as a cultural system that promotes the apparent dissolution of obligation. Wage labor is a cultural concept, as is the related concept of profits, and both concepts encourage those who earn money to think of their earnings as reflecting their individual efforts, and therefore as theirs alone to spend. When Marx analyzed the wage labor relationship, however, he was less interested in exploring what it encouraged people to imagine than in the miseries it caused. He argued, for example, that the wage worker is alienated *(a)* from his product, which belongs to his employer, *(b)* from himself because he must follow his employer's orders rather than decide for himself what to do, *(c)* from his humanity in that he cannot exercise his human capacity for planning, and *(d)* from his fellows in that capitalist competition encourages him to see others as means to his own ends rather than as fellow humans.[10] This last form of alienation comes closest to Durkheim's concept of the cult of the individual. Capitalist competition for wages and profits encourages those who engage in it to apply cost-benefit analyses to their personal relationships as well as to their market transactions.

Although Durkheim was right in predicting the evolution of human rights documents and in identifying rampant selfishness as a major problem of modern society, he was wrong in his assumption that the development of human rights documents such as the UDHR would lead to more equitable social relations. Durkheim's vision of the just society may have been partly realized in the industrialized welfare states established after World War II. But since at least the OPEC oil cri-

---

10. Karl Marx, "Estranged Labor," in *The Marx-Engels Reader,* 2d. ed., ed. Robert C. Tucker (New York: W. W. Norton, 1978), 70. See also Bertell Ollman, *Alienation: Marx's Conception of Man in Capitalist Society* (Cambridge: Cambridge University Press, 1971).

sis of the early 1970s, the gap between rich and poor nations—as well as the gap between rich and poor people within nations—seems to be growing. At the end of the twentieth century, the "advent of a world in which human beings shall enjoy . . . freedom from fear and want" (to say nothing of freedom of speech and belief) seemed as far—if not farther—from realization as it did when Durkheim wrote at the end of the nineteenth century.

One reason why Durkheim may have been wrong to imagine that human rights documents would lead to more equitable social relations was that he used legal codes as visible manifestations of the invisible moral orders he wanted to study and compare. Because, he argued, "social solidarity is a completely moral phenomenon which, taken by itself does not lend itself to exact observation nor indeed to measurement," he decided to "substitute for this internal fact which escapes us an external index which symbolizes it and study the former in the light of the latter. This visible symbol is law" (64). But by treating law as an external symbol for the moral phenomena that he thought actually regulated human action, Durkheim deprived himself of the conceptual tools needed to study the gap between law on the books and law in action. If law were a mere outward symbol for morality, there could be no systemic gap between what the law told people to do and what people actually did.

Anthropologists, of course, have long recognized that Durkheim got his legal systems backward. The "primitive" societies that were supposed to have repressive sanctions, reflecting people's collective horror of wrongdoing, actually tend to have the restitutive sanctions that Durkheim associated with contractual solidarity. And modern industrialized states with complex divisions of labor tend to have impressive prison systems for incarcerating poor wrongdoers rather than enabling them to repay those they harmed. But Durkheim's argument that modern society requires restitutive sanctions may not be as misplaced as seems at first glance. It does, however, need to be supplemented by a concern for incentives. When Malinowski described the law of "savages" in the Trobriand Islands as based on reciprocity, he suggested that reciprocity was enforced not merely by restitutive sanctions but also by inducements to comply.[11] I will return to the

---

11. Bronislaw Malinowski, *Crime and Custom in Savage Society* (London: Kegan Paul, Trench and Trubner, 1926).

question of inducements at the end of this essay, after I have considered cultural relativist arguments against the spread of universal human rights.

As should be obvious from my discussion of Durkheim, I agree with those who argue that human rights is a Western discourse.[12] I do not think that human rights are universal in the sense of being common to all cultures. Not only am I unconvinced by efforts to prove that all cultures respect human dignity and deplore interpersonal violence,[13] but I think that efforts to find such equivalences—however well intentioned—are misguided.[14] It is precisely because moral discourses of human rights and economic discourses of capitalism are both products of the post-Enlightenment West that we need to analyze the relationship between them if we are to assess the usefulness of human rights discourses for tempering the selfish disregard for others that capitalism encourages.[15]

There is good evidence that the Western concept of human rights is foreign to many people who are now being exposed to the idea. In Chiapas, Mexico, where I have been doing anthropological field work since 1960, the Zapatista uprising of January 1994 brought many human rights organizations to the region. The central city of San Cristobal de Las Casas now houses offices of the Mexican national and Chiapas state human rights commissions, as well as an organization affiliated with the Catholic Church and several other human rights NGOs. Nevertheless, it is clear that many people, particularly those from indigenous Maya communities, interpret human rights in ways that do not coincide with Western understandings.

Christine Kovic, an anthropologist who worked with the Catholic

---

12. Charles Taylor, "Human Rights: The Legal Culture," in *International Human Rights in Context*, ed. Henry J. Steiner and Philip Alston (Oxford: Clarendon Press, 1948), 173–76; and R. Pannikar, "Is the Notion of Human Rights a Western Concept?" in *Law and Anthropology*, ed. P. Sack and J. Aleck (Aldershot: Dartmouth, 1992).

13. Alison Dundes Renteln, "Relativism and the Search for Human Rights," *American Anthropologist* 90 (1988): 56. See also W. Penn Handwerker, "Universal Human Rights and the Problem of Unbounded Cultural Meanings," *American Anthropologist* 99 (1997): 799.

14. See Jack Donnelly, *Universal Human Rights in Theory and Practice* (Ithaca: Cornell University Press, 1989); and Wilson, "Human Rights." I do appreciate the fact that if an investigator is able to show that groups who claim to have a non-Western culture have their own version of human rights, the task of trying to hold "non-Western" political leaders to human rights moral principles will be made easier.

15. Pannikar, "Notion of Human Rights."

human rights organization and who recently completed a dissertation on human rights in the region, reports that in

> Tzotzil [one of the local Maya languages] there is no word which directly translates as rights as they are understood in a Western-European tradition. Rights are understood as responsibilities rather than entitlements. For example, in an interview in a Tzotzil community that had recently suffered numerous human rights violations related to land conflict, we asked an elder what "right" the *campesino* [peasant] had to land. He responded, "The *campesino* has the right to care for the land" and then he proceeded to talk of the importance of not burning the land nor using fertilizer.[16]

A similar vision of rights as responsibilities occurred when human rights workers asked members of another indigenous community about the human right to adequate food. Instead of stressing their own entitlement to nourishment, those who were questioned replied that they had "the right to share the little food that we have with people who need it."[17]

Jan Rus, another anthropologist who works in the region, told me that when he and several Tzotzil speakers tried to translate a North American document about the human rights of migrant workers, they had to give up after being unable to come up with Tzotzil phrasing that meant anything other than that people had the right to do as they pleased without interference from the authorities.[18] And in my own research in the Tzotzil community of Zinacantán, I have been finding that people refer to human rights primarily in the context of getting out of jail. One man, for example, when I asked him about *derechos humanos,* told me that it had to do with people who helped you if you had been imprisoned. "They will help you even if you have no money," he assured me. Indeed, all the references except one to human rights in the Zinacanteco judicial archives of 1996 occurred in letters written to state

---

16. Christine Kovic, "Walking with One Heart: Human Rights and the Catholic Church among the Maya of Highland Chiapas," Ph.D. diss., City University of New York, 1997, 101–2.

17. Ibid., 102.

18. Jan Rus, personal communication.

and national human rights commissions asking for help in securing the release of prisoners.[19]

Given that Western discourses of human rights are alien to many cultures, it may seem surprising that I, as an anthropologist who respects cultural differences, am not more alarmed by the spread of human rights discourses around the world.[20] One reason I am less worried than I might be is that the moral discourse of human rights is a language of argument. If human rights violations were always punished by the use of repressive force, then one might have reason to worry about imposing human rights on social groups for whom the concept is alien. But human rights are not always enforced. Not only is the international community loath to interfere in the supposedly internal affairs of nation-states,[21] but there are wide disagreements on just which rights should be universally recognized. There are also ordinary, everyday disagreements over what constitutes a violation of human rights. In Chiapas, for example, incidents that the Catholic Church human rights organization denounces as "torture" are proclaimed by the Mexican National Commission on Human Rights to be mere abuses of authority by security forces. The human right not to be "subjected to torture" (Article 5 of the UDHR) may be one of the most widely accepted human rights, in contrast to the economic, social, and cultural rights that are widely disputed. But there is still considerable disagreement over what constitutes torture.[22]

More important, human rights discourses contain internal contradictions.[23] The major reason why I, as an anthropologist, do not join those who deplore the spread of Western human rights discourses is that the apparent contradiction between advocating universal human

19. The one letter to a state human rights commission that did not ask for the release of a prisoner was written by an old man who asked for relief from persecution by the adult children he had disinherited.

20. Anthropologists do have a tradition of criticizing the notion of universal human rights as Western and ethnocentric. In 1947, the American Anthropological Association opposed the Universal Declaration of Human Rights on the grounds that it did not recognize cultural difference.

21. Linda Bosniak, "Human Rights, State Sovereignty, and the Protection of Undocumented Migrants under the International Migrant Workers Convention," *International Migration Review* 25 (1991): 737.

22. Talal Asad, "On Torture, or Cruel, Inhuman, and Degrading Treatment," in Wilson, *Human Rights*, 111.

23. Cheah, "Posit(ion)ing Human Rights."

rights and respecting cultural differences is not a contradiction between cultural traditions but rather one within the Western discourse of human rights itself.[24] The argument that peoples should be allowed to develop their own legal traditions makes sense only within a discourse of rights that grants peoples the right to self-determination (Article 1 of the International Covenant of Civil and Political Rights). The very idea that peoples should be able to decide for themselves which laws will govern them, rather than submitting to the laws of God or to laws laid down by their conquerors, is a product of the European Enlightenment. I thus believe that it does not make sense to ask if human rights can be advanced without thwarting efforts to develop indigenous legal traditions. In the contemporary world, indigenous peoples are developing their legal traditions in the context of human rights discourses.[25]

It is true that in the past (and perhaps in the present), peoples who were outside the orbit of European expansion or marginal to capitalist economic regimes did develop "legal systems" reflecting their own cultural values and concerns. I found, for example, that the Zinacantecos I studied in the 1960s based their handling of interpersonal conflicts on an understanding of human and cosmic nature that was very different from that of the post-Enlightenment West.[26] At that time, the community of Zinacantán was largely left alone to manage its own affairs. The Mexican state rarely interfered in Zinacanteco political organization, and the Zinacanteco economy was peripheral to capitalism. Today, however, after the worldwide economic shifts set in motion by the OPEC oil crisis, Zinacantecos participate in capitalist market relations and Zinacanteco leaders belong to national political parties.[27] The Zapatista rebellion of 1994 has also flooded the state of Chiapas with secu-

24. Thomas Hylland Eriksen, "Multiculturalism, Individualism, and Human Rights: Romanticism, the Enlightenment, and Lessons from Mauritius," in Wilson, *Human Rights,* 49.

25. Wilson, "Human Rights." Also Sally Engle Merry, "Legal Pluralism and Transnational Culture: The Ka Ho'okolokolonui Kanaka Maoli Tribunal, Hawai'i, 1993," in Wilson, *Human Rights,* 28.

26. Jane F. Collier, *Law and Social Change in Zinacantan* (Stanford, Calif.: Stanford University Press, 1973).

27. George Collier, *Basta: Land and the Zapatista Rebellion in Chiapas,* 2d ed. (Oakland, Calif.: Food First Books, 1999). See also Frank Cancian, *The Decline of Community in Zinacantan: Economy, Public Life, and Social Stratification* (Stanford, Calif.: Stanford University Press, 1992).

rity forces and human rights workers. Today, when Zinacanteco leaders and leaders of other Maya communities assert their right to practice their "indigenous customs," they do so in the context of Western discourses of human rights. Such leaders are claiming—quite consciously—their "universal human right" as indigenous peoples to self-determination.

There is a famous case from another indigenous community in Chiapas that illustrates the tension between cultural relativism and universalism that is internal to the Western discourse of human rights. Since the Mexican debt crisis of the 1980s, authorities in several indigenous communities, but particularly Chamula, have expelled many people for being "Protestants," claiming that their religious conversion threatened local customs and traditions. These expulsions were in obvious violation not only of universal human rights doctrines, but also of Mexico's own constitutional guarantee of religious freedom. The large number of people expelled led to a political crisis, and in 1992 the state legislature of Chiapas convened a public hearing on the problem. At this hearing, a Chamula leader, Enrique Gomez Patishtan, invoked the right of peoples to self-determination to defend the expulsion of Protestants:

> As indigenous peoples, we want to be taken into account when laws are made, because this has never happened. We cannot accept that the Protestants make fun of our images and our saints in the church, and then they insult our sacraments, which we consider are sacred and teach our children. Therefore, we believe that customs and traditions should define the law and not the reverse.[28]

Although Chamula authorities and the national press portrayed the expulsions as due to religious conflict, others have argued—convincingly, in my view—that the expulsions occurred for political and economic reasons. Not only were several of the people who were expelled not Protestants at the time of their expulsion, but many of them belonged to a political party that had opposed the ruling municipal authorities in the last election. The ruling clique in Chamula, who controlled both municipal political offices and lucrative economic

---

28. Congreso del Estado de Chiapas, 1992, quoted in Kovic, "Walking with One Heart," 119.

monopolies, were expelling their opponents.[29] This story of politically and economically motivated expulsions, however, went largely unheard, primarily because the Chamula authorities who carried out the expulsions were supporters of, and supported by, Mexico's national ruling party, the PRI.[30]

Because the contradiction between universal human rights and respect for cultural differences is internal to human rights discourses, the tension between universalism and relativism is not going to go away. It is, in fact, likely to become more acute as indigenous peoples, who were once able to govern themselves in relative isolation, are increasingly participating in capitalist economic relations and "democratizing" political regimes. Today, indigenous peoples who demand political autonomy are usually appealing to universal human rights in order to claim a right to self-determination.[31] But even as they appeal to the Western discourse of universal human rights to claim self-determination, they simultaneously reject the claim of human rights to be a universal discourse. They assert instead their right to develop their own culturally distinct political and legal traditions. In Chiapas, at least, many people regard this tension between universalism and relativism as a productive one. They do not want it resolved in favor of either position.

Many of those who favor political autonomy for indigenous groups in Chiapas want to retain the idea of universal human rights, both to justify the right of indigenous peoples to self-determination and to protect the rights of individuals from potentially oppressive laws passed by indigenous councils. Indigenous women and their supporters have been particularly articulate in arguing both sides of the contradiction. For example, the document summarizing the consensus reached in the Zapatista-organized roundtable on "justice and human rights in the democratic transition" supports the right of indigenous

---

29. Kovic, "Walking with One Heart."

30. Cases like this one tend to confirm what many critics of cultural relativism have pointed out: that the most vocal supporters of cultural relativism, who denounce universal human rights as another example of Western imperialism, are often not powerless people seeking relief from oppression but local elites trying to retain their privileges (Donnelly, *Universal Human Rights*). Nevertheless, there are many instances, such as is occurring in Zinacantan, where the efforts of indigenous leaders to demand legal autonomy from the state are actually benefiting less fortunate community members.

31. Wilson, "Human Rights."

communities *(pueblos indios)* "to determine their political organization, elect their political and judicial authorities, and practice their own norms and ways of imparting justice" even as it requires that "all the fundamental human rights of women" be protected and guaranteed within indigenous communities.[32] Similarly, a proposal for "amplifying" the Zapatista-inspired "revolutionary law of women," which is largely concerned with asserting women's universal human right to equal participation in political and economic affairs, concludes with the assertion that "women have the right to be respected in their use of traditional customs, languages, and regional dress."[33] Ironically, but not unexpectedly, people trying to deal with the problem of reconciling indigenous autonomy with universal human rights seem to be coming up with the formula developed by turn-of-the-century colonialists advocating indirect rule for colonized peoples: The idea that indigenous peoples should be free to practice their own customs as long as these are not repugnant to the moral sensibilities of post-Enlightenment Westerners.[34]

Although I do not support the cultural relativist position against the spread of universal human rights, those who argue for cultural relativism have raised at least two important issues that need to be addressed. First, they are right to be skeptical about the real accom-

---

32. In Spanish, proposal C under "derechos y cultura indígena" reads: "autodeterminar su forma de organización politica interna, elegir sus autoridades políticas y judiciales, utilizar sus propios sistemas normativos y de impartición de justicia." Proposal A under proposals for the rights of women reads: "Exigimos que se garanticen y protejan todos los derechos humanos de la mujer: sus derechos fundamentales; los civiles y políticos; los económicos sociales y culturales; y su derecho a no ser discriminada por cuestiones de género. Estos derechos también deben garantizarse en las comunidades indígenas y campesinas." (This is a document that I acquired in typescript from friends in Chiapas.)

33. In Spanish, Article 33 of the "propuesta de ampliación de la ley revolucionaria de mujeres" reads: "Las mujeres tienen derecho a ser respetadas sus usos y costumbres tradicionales, culturales, lenguas y derecho a usar sus trajes regionales." (This is a typescript document that I acquired in Chiapas from friends.)

34. Magdalena Gomez, in an unpublished essay assessing the outcome of the debate over indigenous law ("derecho indigena") between representatives of the Zapatistas and the Mexican government, concludes with a series of possible agreements. Among them are the idea that indigenous councils should have jurisdiction over local affairs and conflicts, but that (1) such councils should be regarded as courts of first instance, whose judgments stand only if not appealed to other authorities, (2) the right of appeal remains open in all cases, and (3) serious crimes ("delitos graves") be handled outside of the indigenous community.

plishments of the Western discourse of human rights.[35] They may not be alone in wondering if modern states are merely paying lip service to human rights while actually becoming more repressive, but they have been active in pointing out that human rights discourses and increasingly efficient state apparatuses of repression seem to be spreading together. Increases in human rights commissions do not seem to be accompanied by decreases in human rights violations. In fact, the reverse may be true.

In the post–Cold War world, human rights commissions and state repression may be increasing together as the triumphant West, through international organizations, is requiring other states to simultaneously enact neoliberal economic reforms and to protect the civil and political rights of citizens. Skeptics correctly point out that economic and political liberalism impose contradictory imperatives, and that the contradiction is usually resolved in favor of economic interests.[36] The "structural adjustment policies" being imposed on debtor states by the International Monetary Fund and the World Bank, for example, along with state policies aimed at stemming capital flight, are working together to benefit the rich at the expense of those who have little or nothing. And as growing social inequality fuels political unrest, increasingly impoverished states are resorting to coercive measures to stifle opposition among populations whose living standards are deteriorating.

The situation in Chiapas can be understood as a product of this process. The roots of the 1994 Zapatista rebellion, and of the low-intensity warfare that continues in the region, can be understood as outcomes of the economic and political policies adopted by the Mexican state to deal with the debt crisis of the 1980s and the resulting structural adjustments required by the international financial community.[37] Before the debt crisis, the Mexican state was able to buy off potential dissidents with policies aimed at helping the poor. But as the state was forced to cut back on social programs, such as building roads, schools, and hospitals, and on providing economic aid for small producers, peasant organizations that had argued for working within the legal

---

35. Bilhari Kausikan, "Asia's Different Standard," *Foreign Policy* 92 (1993): 24.

36. Steven Lukes, "Is There an Alternative to Market Utopianism?" in *The New Great Transformation? Change and Continuity in East-Central Europe,* ed. Christopher Bryant and E. Mokrzycki (New York: Routledge, 1994).

37. Collier, *Basta.*

framework of the state lost their ability to provide benefits for their supporters. At the same time, the Mexican state, faced with increasing unrest in the countryside, strengthened its repressive forces. The Chiapas state government, for example, "reformed" the state penal code in ways that many people have argued violated universal human rights to freedom of assembly and expression, and to freedom from arbitrary imprisonment. Finally, the Mexican state, recognizing the growing political unrest in Chiapas, poured money into the region. But because structural adjustment policies prevented the state from using money in ways that could really help the poor, the state ended up spending the money on security forces and on subsidies for those who supported the ruling party. The money thus contributed to growing political unrest by militarizing the region and by widening the gap between the powerful rich and the powerless poor. Peasant farmers, who found themselves increasingly marginalized, and with legal channels for redress increasingly cut off, flocked to organizations, such as the Zapatistas, that advocated armed rebellion. Many dispossessed peasants, for example, found themselves agreeing with the Zapatista statement that as they were going to die of hunger anyway, they might as well die fighting.

In the aftermath of the debt crisis, as the Mexican state became increasingly repressive, it also created, for the first time in its history, a national human rights commission to investigate supposed violations. The commission, which many critics assumed was created to please the United States and to cover up embarrassing situations, has been more independent than its critics feared.[38] But officials linked to the government continue to hinder the investigation of human rights violations, particularly in Chiapas. In the fall of 1997, for example, the head of an international commission on human rights was prohibited from visiting the state, which is reported to have the highest rate of human rights violations of any state in Mexico. And within Chiapas, the immigration authorities have been active in expelling foreigners who come to work with local human rights NGOs. While no one can doubt that international concern for protecting human rights, along with the willingness of independent organizations to publicize violations, have encouraged the Mexican government to avoid repressive actions against the Zap-

---

38. Yves Dezalay and Bryant Garth, "Building the Law and Putting the State into Play: International Strategies among Mexico's Divided Elite," American Bar Foundation Working Paper no. 9509 (1997).

atistas that might incur international condemnation, the government has also refrained from taking positive measures to promote peace in the region. In particular, the government has failed to reign in local supporters, such as the paramilitary group that carried out the massacre of Zapatista sympathizers in Acteal on December 22, 1997.

Just as supporters of cultural relativism are right to question the effectiveness of universal human rights, so they are right to ask whether the Western discourse of human rights, which encodes Western individualism, is appropriate for cultures where people stress obligations to others over the rights of individuals.[39] Supporters of cultural relativism may acknowledge that rights and obligations are not mutually exclusive: individual rights do impose an obligation on others to respect those rights. But they are also correct to point out that obligations in liberal political theory are generally of the negative kind—the obligation not to interfere with others' freedom—rather than the positive obligation to ensure others' well-being.

Supporters of universal human rights, in opposing this critique of Western individualism, have commonly observed that liberal political theory has evolved over time. Whereas seventeenth- and eighteenth-century European philosophers may have stressed the rights of individuals against society, later theorists, such as Durkheim, have stressed society's obligation to ensure that all individuals have access to the social and material resources they need to exercise free choice. Supporters of universal human rights point to such documents as the International Covenant on Economic, Social, and Cultural Rights, which requires states to create conditions whereby everyone may experience life with dignity. This covenant may not enjoy the widespread support of the International Covenant on Civil and Political Rights, but it is a product of the Western discourse of human rights.

In this debate over the applicability of universal human rights to societies that stress obligations, I side with supporters of cultural relativism. They are right to argue that the Western discourse of universal human rights is not appropriate for cultures where obligations to others take precedence over the rights of individuals. The problem, how-

---

39. See Robert Cover, "Obligation: A Jewish Jurisprudence of the Social Order," *Journal of Law and Religion* 5 (1987): 65: and Abdullahi A. An-Na'im, *Human Rights in Cross-Cultural Perspectives: A Quest for Consensus* (Philadelphia: University of Pennsylvania Press, 1992).

ever, is that such obligations-based social systems seem to be rapidly disappearing.[40]

When I refer to obligations-based social systems, I do not mean cultures that merely voice a commitment to obligations. Rather, I have in mind socioeconomic systems in which real rewards of power, prestige, and privilege accrue to those who can claim to be sacrificing themselves for others. These are socioeconomic systems such as the one Malinowski observed in the Trobriand Islands early in this century, where those who gave away more than was required by their existing obligations could acquire increased power, prestige, and privilege.[41] It is these kinds of social systems that seem to be disappearing from the contemporary world as peoples whose economies were once marginal to capitalism join the capitalist market for jobs and commodities.[42]

My field research over thirty years in two rural communities, one in Chiapas and one in southern Spain,[43] has convinced me that while cultural rhetorics of obligation may survive and even flourish with ethnic revivals, the material rewards accruing to apparent self-sacrifice tend to evaporate as people participate in capitalist markets. The renewed spread of capitalist market relations around the world is dissolving human ties of obligation, just as Marx said it would, jeopardizing the well-being of those who find it difficult to make a living in the capitalist market because they have no capital and there are no jobs, or because employers refuse to hire people who are too young, too old, too infirm, or too burdened with caring for family members to be good workers.

Although I observed the dissolution of obligations-based social systems in both Spain and Chiapas, I will continue to draw examples from Chiapas to describe how one such system worked, and to explain why and how peoples' incorporation into capitalist market relations

---

40. Donnelly, *Universal Human*, 118.

41. Malinowski, *Crime and Custom*.

42. Obligations-based social systems do seem to be disappearing at the present time as the capitalist market expands by turning ever more of the world's resources into commodities. But it is possible to imagine that a global recession could lead to a retraction of the market and so to the reconstruction of obligations-based social systems. The people in such systems, however, are likely to be poor and marginalized. Powerful participants in capitalist markets usually allow only those resources they regard as relatively worthless to escape commodification.

43. Jane Collier, *From Duty to Desire: Remaking Families in a Spanish Village* (Princeton: Princeton University Press, 1997).

shifted rewards from those who took care of others to those who took care of themselves.

When I first did fieldwork in the Tzotzil-speaking Maya community of Zinacantán in the 1960s, the most powerful and prestigious people were men who could claim to be sacrificing themselves for the good of others. The richest and most powerful man in Zinacantán, for example, routinely dressed in rags as a potent symbol of the fact that he had given everything away. All of his money was out in interest-free loans (but could, of course, be called back rapidly should he need cash), and he spent all of his time serving his community in various ritual and political offices (while other members of his household farmed his corn, cooked his meals, washed his clothes, and so forth).

In the 1960s, Zinacantán was a community where labor was the scarce factor in production. Zinacantecos were primarily corn farmers, growing their own food and selling the surplus. Land was available to all at modest rents, and Zinacantecos used simple tools that were cheap to buy. As a result, those who were able to farm the most corn, and so produce the largest harvests, tended to be those who could accumulate the most labor in their households.[44] A system of marriage with bridewealth, in which grooms were required to "repay" the parents of brides for the expenses of raising a daughter, ensured that young men worked for elders who could help them marry. And a system of religious offices, in which men paid to serve the saints, created a distinction between successful elders who had accumulated the ritual knowledge needed to speak with the gods, and elders whose failure to take religious posts condemned to having to ask others to speak to the gods for them. In short, Zinacantán in the 1960s was a community where men who had "sacrificed themselves" by using their money to help bachelors marry and to serve the saints could accumulate many workers in their households and many followers to do their bidding. In contrast, those who were condemned to act "selfishly," such as young men who needed brides and people who had to eat their share of the harvest because it was too small to give any away, lacked the prestige and power enjoyed by those who "generously" shared with others.

Even though women and young men could not aspire to the prestige and power enjoyed by older men who "gave everything away," women and young men could exercise the power that came with elder

---

44. Frank Cancian, *Economics and Prestige in a Maya Community* (Stanford, Calif.: Stanford University Press, 1965).

men's need for their labor and cooperation. Because elders needed young men to work for them, powerful elders did help young men to acquire the wives and ritual knowledge that enabled young men to become successful elders in turn. And because men needed women to prepare food for farm laborers, do the housework, and produce the children who would become future workers, men who aspired to become heads of large households had to pay attention to women's wishes and to provide for women's children. It was also true that while women had fewer opportunities than men to give things away, older women who successfully managed large households and who had acquired ritual knowledge while serving in religious posts with their husbands could enjoy almost as much respect and power as senior men.

By the mid-1980s, however, economic changes had undermined the rewards of apparent self-sacrifice. During Mexico's oil boom of the 1970s, when a surge in construction increased the number of wage jobs available to unskilled workers, Zinacanteco grooms escaped having to serve their elders by eloping with brides and then paying the bride's parents with cash they earned. As a result, elder farmers found themselves without a youthful labor force and so started replacing labor with purchased inputs: chemical weed killers to replace hoe weeding, and fertilizers to replace the cutting and burning of new fields. By the time world oil prices fell in the 1980s, and Mexico's economic boom gave way to economic bust and the debt crisis, Zinacantán had already become a community where capital had replaced labor as the scarce factor in production. As structural adjustment policies did away with wage jobs, and unemployed Zinacanteco men started returning to their community, they returned to a changed farming system: one where those who had money to buy commercial weed killers and fertilizers could farm corn, whereas those who lacked money—even if they had land—had to work as wage laborers for others.[45] No longer did Zinacanteco men earn power, prestige, and wealth by giving everything away. Quite the contrary. Today people who have money benefit by avoiding as many community and family obligations as possible. The rich prefer to lend their money out at interest rather than giving interest-free loans to needy kin and neighbors. They also prefer to invest in capital goods, such as trucks or market stalls, rather than to spend their money serving the saints. And instead of trying to accumu-

45. Collier, *Basta*.

late many workers and potential workers in their households, men who earn money understandably tend to regard their wives, children, and elderly parents as economic liabilities who consume more than they contribute.

Zinacantecos often characterize the economic changes they experienced as a shift in people's motivations from "seeking food" to "seeking money."[46] In the old days—they say—family members worked together for food. Today, people want money. I, of course, follow Marx in attributing this shift less to people having changed their individual hierarchy of desires than to a shift in the economic system that altered the distribution of rewards, thus changing what it made sense for people to want if they hoped to earn the respect of their fellows. In the 1960s, those who sought food could aspire to the wealth, prestige, and power that came from having large households and large harvests to give away. In the 1980s and 1990s, those who were successful in seeking money could buy not only the capital goods needed for production, but also the consumer goods that demonstrated wealth and power in a social system now divided primarily by class rather than by age and sex.

I also follow Marx in attributing the apparent selfishness that accompanies capitalism less to a high division of labor that isolates people from one another than to people's experiences of market relations. The competition that capitalism sets up between capitalists for profits and between workers for jobs encourages people to experience the money they earn as being paid to them for their own efforts. And when people imagine that they earn money all by themselves, it makes sense for them assume that they also earn the right to decide how that money should be spent.

Between June and December 1997, I attended the local court in Zinacantán, exploring, among other things, the effects of this assumption on family conflicts and their resolution. The changes I observed since the 1960s are subtle, but I think profound. In 1997, as in the 1960s, marital disputes comprised the overwhelming majority of cases handled by municipal judges. But there was a shift in who initiated cases. In the 1960s, most marital disputes were brought to court by young husbands and their kin seeking the return of wives who had run away. In those days, husbands had to recover their wives and children if they were to have households to head. Indeed, men who could not convince

---

46. George Collier, "Seeking Food and Seeking Money: Changing Productive Relations in a Highland Mexican Community," Discussion Paper 11 (Geneva: United Nations Research Institute for Social Development, 1990).

a woman to marry them could not remain in Zinacantán. In 1997, husbands still initiated cases, but most marital disputes seemed to be brought to court by runaway wives and their kin who wanted husbands to fulfill marital obligations.

In 1997, as in the 1960s, most runaway wives said they wanted a divorce, and most marital disputes ended in reconciliation rather than separation. Husbands usually begged pardon from their wives and asked them to return home. But I noticed significant changes in how young husbands behaved in court and in the arguments that mediators used to secure a reconciliation. In the 1960s, young husbands often knelt or sat silently while their senior kin apologized for them to the wife's senior kin. In the recent cases, in contrast, many young husbands behaved defiantly and appeared reluctant to beg a wife's pardon. Instead of acting mutely miserable, husbands angrily complained of nagging wives who did nothing but ask for money. And when husbands were finally convinced to beg pardon, they commonly mumbled apologies and tried to escape as rapidly as possible. The most significant change, however, occurred in mediators' arguments. Elders in the 1960s mouthed platitudes about how husbands and wives needed one another. In the court cases I observed recently, in contrast, judges tried to convince young husbands to seek reconciliation by telling them that if they did get a divorce, they would have to give monthly child support payments to their wives and sign documents guaranteeing the children's right to inherit land, trucks, and so forth.

These changes reflect the economic shift from seeking food to seeking money. In the 1960s, it was clear to everyone that young men needed the cooperation of their wives and children if they were to become successful heads of large households. Today, however, a young man has good reason to wonder whether he might gain more advantage by investing his hard-earned money in capital goods such as a truck, or in prestige goods such as a television set or new cowboy boots, than in food and medicine for his wife and children, particularly if his wife criticizes him and his children keep getting sick.[47] Moreover, given women's need for money and their lack of opportunities for earning it, a man can easily acquire a replacement wife if he decides that his present one is not worth the money he spends on her.

47. The case I found most disturbing was one in which a husband divorced his wife for adultery and kept their elder children. Although his wife denied the accusation, the fact that she had accepted money from another man to buy medicine for her sick baby was taken as proof that she had slept with her benefactor in return.

As should be obvious, this economic shift has had a devastating effect on women and children—and the elderly. In the 1960s, when family members worked together for food, a wife's work in cooking, washing, weaving, and childcare appeared as vital to provisioning the household as her husband's work in the cornfields. Their equal contributions were reflected in an equal division of the harvest should a married couple divorce. Today, however, when money has become more important than family labor, the work that women do in their households has become valueless because it does not earn money. This became painfully clear to me as I watched marital disputes in 1997. Whereas women in the 1960s used to claim a share in the family's resources by citing the work that they did (and many wives still try to make such claims), it is obvious that women's work has become legally irrelevant. No longer is it men's need for women's household labor that prompts a husband to ensure his wife's well-being. Rather, it is now the state that tries to force husbands to support their wives and children. Written birth certificates have become vital documents for ensuring a child's (and therefore the child's mother's) right to share a man's earnings. (I suspect, however, that Zinacanteco authorities are having as little success collecting child-support payments from divorced fathers as U.S. authorities have in collecting from deadbeat dads. In Zinacantán, as in the rest of the world, single mothers and their young children are the poorest of the poor.)[48]

I began this essay by agreeing with Durkheim that universal human rights is the appropriate moral discourse for modern capitalist society. Because people's participation in capitalist market relations leads them to experience their earnings as paid them as individuals for the work that they do, people have good reason to imagine that rights are more important than obligations. After all, it is individuals' right to dispose of their bodies and property that appears to determine their incomes in the market for jobs and commodities. It thus makes sense for those who participate in capitalist market relations not only to want their civil and political rights protected, but also to imagine—quoting

---

48. Although I may appear to blame men for the plight of single mothers and their young children, I do not. The economic shift from seeking food to seeking money has hurt Zinacanteco men as well as women. Young men whose families do not already own trucks or market stalls have a hard time finding jobs that pay enough to support a family. Tragically, it seems that joining a paramilitary group and engaging in an illegal activity, such as dealing drugs or smuggling workers into the United States, are the most lucrative occupations open to young men from indigenous communities in highland Chiapas.

the preamble of the International Covenant on Economic, Social, and Cultural Rights—that "the ideal of free human beings enjoying freedom from fear and want can only be achieved if conditions are created whereby everyone may enjoy his economic, social and cultural rights, as well as his civil and political rights."

But if it is easy to understand how capitalism, as an economic system, encourages people to embrace the moral ideals expressed in the UDHR and other human rights documents, it is harder to understand how the moral ideals of human rights can modify capitalist competition to actually create a world in which people enjoy the freedom from fear and want that permits consensual contracts rather than forced ones. Durkheim's vision that law reflected reality was flawed. The existence of human rights documents has not produced a global system in which all people can live with dignity. The two mid-twentieth-century experiments aimed at promoting more equitable social relations by regulating the capitalist market—the welfare state and Communism—both succumbed to increasing capitalist competition at end of the century. Whether these experiments failed because handouts to the poor and state control over the economy discouraged productivity by promoting idleness and dependence, as some critics have charged, or whether they failed because technical and legal developments undermined the ability of states to control capital flows across their borders, the fact remains that neither experiment provides a model for regulating a capitalist market that transcends national boundaries. As Durkheim would have recognized, global capitalism requires global regulations.

A system of global regulations does seem to be developing. Transnational financial institutions, international trade agreements, and meetings among financial ministers are gradually producing regulations to define and protect the property rights required for capitalism to function. At the same time, transnational human rights organizations are working to promote adherence to the moral ideals expressed in human rights documents. Although many human rights activists lament the inability of the international community to punish those who violate the human rights of others, an understanding of how systems based on obligations actually work suggests that perhaps such laments are misguided. Instead of trying to develop ways to punish violators, those who hope to promote universal human rights might do better to look for ways of rewarding—with real power and privilege in addition to medals and honor—those whose actions promote more equitable social relations. Given the Western tendency to think of legal regulations as enforced by sanctions on those who violate them, it may be hard for advocates of human rights to imagine regulations that provide substantive rewards, as well as symbolic ones, for those who go out of their way to promote the human dignity of others. But at the present historical moment, trying to imagine rewards may repay the effort.

The Legal Protection of Human Rights in Africa: How to Do More with Less

Abdullahi A. An-Na'im

It may sound heretical for me as a lawyer to suggest that African societies may actually "do more" for the implementation of human rights "with less" reliance on the legal protection of these rights.[1] My basic argument for this proposition is premised on a dilemma: the importance of legal protection of human rights, on the one hand, and the inability (not simply unwillingness, which is also usually true) of the postcolonial African state to provide adequate legal protection as required by the modern human rights paradigm,[2] on the other. This dilemma leads me to ask: Since the postcolonial state in Africa is unable to provide the necessary legal protection of human rights, should efforts to realize these rights therefore focus on nonlegal strategies of implementation? Indeed, will legal protection ever be appropriate for

---

I am grateful to Professor Rosalind Hackett of the University of Tennessee, Knoxville, for her very valuable critical comments and useful suggestions on the first draft of this chapter.

1. As explained in section II, this chapter is based on studies done in fourteen African countries: Botswana, Egypt, Ethiopia, Ghana, Kenya, Morocco, Mozambique, Nigeria, Rwanda, Senegal, South Africa, Sudan, Uganda, and Zambia. Accordingly, I am not claiming that my analysis here applies to every African country or society, though my basic thesis can probably be substantiated with reference to most of them.

2. By *human rights paradigm* I mean the notion that because certain standards of human rights are binding on states as a matter of international law, protection and implementation is a matter of legitimate international concern, not left exclusively to the domestic jurisdiction of individual states. The binding nature of international human rights norms and an evaluation of the efficacy of international mechanisms for their implementation are not within the ambit of this chapter.

the type and degree of human rights violations experienced by the peoples of Africa today?

In exploring these questions I do not mean to suggest that legal protection of human rights should be abandoned. On the contrary, by the phrase "do more with less" I mean that African states and human rights advocates should keep trying to achieve the maximum possible degree of legal protection with the capacity and resources available to them, as well as seek to realize more implementation of human rights through other strategies. In this chapter, the term *implementation* refers to a proactive deployment of a variety of measures and policies to achieve the actual realization of human rights, and the term *protection* signifies the application of legal enforcement methods in response to specific violations of human rights norms in individual cases. While exploring both approaches, I will argue that implementation is more appropriate in most African countries. That is, I am emphasizing the need to address the structural, cultural, and other root causes of violations in order to implement human rights in a systematic and comprehensive manner, instead of seeking redress for violations on a case-by-case basis. But since legal protection of human rights, in the broader, more inclusive, and accessible sense discussed below, should be part of this emphasis on implementation strategies, what I am suggesting in this chapter may not be so heretical after all.

To begin with a brief explanation of my thesis here, I first note that it is difficult to generalize about the causes and consequences of the decolonization of Africa in the present limited space except to emphasize that there are certain associations between specific global phenomena of the period after World War II, on the one hand, and the untenableness of direct colonial rule, on the other.[3] For my purposes here, I suggest that, in conceding to decolonization, the colonial powers were simply adapting to new trends in global economic and security relations in ways that were more consistent with the internal conditions within those powers than the retention of direct control over their African colonies. This is not to say that human rights were irrelevant even from the perspective of the colonial powers themselves. Rather, it is only to note that human rights were cited by European powers in conceding to the independence of the African colonies, but those con-

---

3. Crawford Young, *The African Colonial State in Comparative Perspective* (New Haven: Yale University Press, 1994), 182–91. See generally John D. Hargreaves, *Decolonization in Africa,* 2d ed. (New York: Longman, 1996).

siderations were subordinate to broader and more compelling economic and political calculations. It is beyond dispute, however, that the human rights dimension of the period after World War II was exploited by African leaders in demanding the end of colonial rule. Consequently, the protection and implementation of human rights became part of the raison d'être of the postcolonial state. However, due to the nature and consequences of colonialism, formal decolonization did not really lead to genuine self-determination. Instead, most postcolonial African states continue to be so dependent on former colonial powers and their allies that they are unable to fulfill their raison d'être of self-determination and implementation of human rights.

Many factors affect the implementation of human rights, such as the level and quality of political commitment, availability of economic resources, activism within civil society, and implementation of administrative, educational, and other policies. However, legal protection is particularly important for the modern paradigm of human rights not only for the judicial enforcement of these rights as legal entitlement, but also to sustain the efficacy and credibility of all other mechanisms and processes relevant to their implementation. The modern paradigm also relies on legal protection as a means for the development and application of operational definitions of rights in relation to other considerations of public policy, as well as for the mediation of competing claims of rights. But, as discussed below, the successful legal protection of rights has its own requirements and conditions. It presupposes a certain degree of political stability, economic resources, institutional capacity, and the willingness and ability of the public at large to resort to the courts for the enforcement of their rights. Legal protection also assumes the prevalence of a certain conception of the rule of law, independence of the judiciary, and executive compliance with judicial determinations.

The lack or weakness of legal protection is an indication of the structural and institutional failure or inadequacy of the system as a whole. For one thing, since access to effective legal remedies is itself a human right, its absence is a violation of human rights. Second, the lack or weakness of legal enforcement is symptomatic of other problems such as executive interference with the independence of the judiciary or failure to comply with its decisions. Problems with the legal enforcement of human rights may be due to underlying cultural and institutional difficulties with the rule of law or evidence of a lack of public confidence in the ability of the courts to vindicate rights that is a reflection of other problems. In other words, one expects weak legal protection of human rights in situations of political instability, economic underdevelopment, institutional incapacity, and the unwillingness or inability of the public at large to resort to the courts for the enforcement of their rights. Whatever the reasons, the lack or weakness of legal protection of human rights means that its functions in the definition and mediation of rights are unfulfilled, leading to even greater weakness of legal protection. Ironically, therefore, legal protection of human rights tends to be weakest where it is most needed. Moreover, a society that needs to do more to implement human rights because it is less able to protect them legally usually faces other serious problems that make it even harder for it to "do more with less" in the sense of addressing root causes of violations.

The objective of this chapter is to examine the nature and implications of this phenomenon in relation to certain African societies today, and to suggest strategies for dealing with this compounded predicament. To pursue this double objective, I first offer a working definition of human rights and a brief analysis of the nature of the postcolonial state in Africa in order to understand the general relationship between the two. Against this background, section II focuses on specific issues of adequate legal protection of human rights in the postcolonial context, with a view to enhancing the prospects of legal protection as such. Finally, section III considers broader issues of structural and cultural factors, as well as political, economic, and social context, with a view to suggesting a strategy for greater implementation of human rights with less reliance on legal protection.

I. Human Rights and the Decolonization/Recolonization of Africa

In articulating a working definition of human rights for the purposes of this chapter, I would begin by emphasizing that human rights are the product of a long history of struggle for social justice and resistance to oppression in all human societies. As Mamdani put it:

> Wherever oppression occurs—and no continent has had a monopoly over this phenomenon in history—there must come into being a conception of rights. . . . This is why it is difficult to accept that

human rights was a theoretical notion created only three centuries ago by philosophers in Europe. True, one can quote Aristotle and his ideological justification of slavery as evidence that the idea of human rights was indeed foreign to the conscience of the ruling classes in ancient Greece. And yet, did anyone—as [Paulin J.] Hountondji rightly asks—question the slaves? Given what we know today of slave revolts in antiquity, can we assume that these in no way shaped the thinking of slaves, such as giving rise to a conception of rights that tended to undermine the legitimacy of their masters' practice? Or, given that no one bothered to hand down to us the victims' discourse on their oppression in ancient Greece, must we assume the opposite?[4]

This does not mean that all human societies have actually articulated and applied human rights in the modern sense of the term, namely as rights that are due to every human being, without distinction on such grounds as gender, race, ethnicity, religion, language, or national origin. The point here is to understand this modern concept of human rights as a specific manifestation of an ancient pursuit of social justice and resistance to oppression by all human societies. That is, the modern concept should be seen as the product of, and building on, earlier conceptions and efforts, rather than a total break with past experiences of human societies around the world. While different societies pursue this objective in accordance with their own political and cultural conditions, there are sufficient similarities of experience and mutual influence to support progression toward shared understandings and common strategies. To emphasize an exclusive claim of some societies to the authorship of the modern concept of human rights undermines the very nature and objectives of these rights as a common cause for all humanity. In my view, this historical perspective is essential for substantiating the universality of human rights: all human societies and communities can identify with the concept and contribute to the specification of its normative content, precisely because it is already part of their own history and current experiences.

It is in this light that one should understand the obvious association between the modern concept of human rights and a particular line

---

4. Mahmood Mamdani, "The Social Basis of Constitutionalism in Africa," *Journal of Modern African Studies* 28, no. 3 (1990): 359–60.

of philosophical and cultural development within West European and North American (herein referred to as Western) societies over the last two to three centuries. The joint authorship by all human societies of the modern concept of human rights can be further elaborated as follows.

First, the Western origin of the modern concept of human rights does not mean that it is accepted by all Western philosophical and ideological perspectives. This concept is the product of a specific line of development in Western thinking and experience and is opposed in its full scope and implications by some aspects of Western thinking and practice.[5] Therefore, one should not assume Western unity in support of the full range of human rights. The very fact that these rights are appealed to in Western societies means that opposition to them remains.

Second, since the modern concept of human rights emerged in the West in response to particular models of political organization and economic development, the same concept would probably provide an appropriate response to the adoption of those models in other societies. That is, because Western models of the extensive and centralized powers of the state and capitalist economic development have been "universalized" through colonialism and its aftermath, the modern idea of human rights that emerged in Western experience in response to those models will probably be necessary for achieving social justice and resisting oppression wherever those models were adopted.[6] For example, trade union rights are necessary for the protection of the human dignity and well-being of workers under certain types of relations of production, wherever those relations may prevail in the world.

Third, to accept the Western origins of the modern concept of human rights, and its linkage to Western political and economic models that now prevail throughout the world, is not to take a determinis-

---

5. See generally, for example, Virginia Leary, "The Effect of Western Perspectives on International Human Rights," in *Human Rights in Africa: Cross-Cultural Perspective*, ed. Abdullahi A. An-Na'im and Francis M. Deng (Washington, D.C.: Brookings Institution, 1990), 15–30; and Virginia Leary, "Postliberal Strands in Western Human Rights Theory: Personalist-Communitarian Perspectives," in *Human Rights in Cross-Cultural Perspectives: Quest for Consensus*, ed. Abdullahi A. An-Na'im (Philadelphia: University of Pennsylvania Press, 1992), 105–32.

6. This point has been made by Rhoda Howard in several articles and developed more fully in *Human Rights and the Search for Community* (Boulder, Colo.: Westview Press, 1995).

tic view of the normative content and the mechanisms of implementation of these rights. Since political and economic models constantly
evolve and adapt to changing conditions everywhere, the precise
nature of corresponding human rights formulations is also likely to
change over time and from one place to another. This is clear enough
from the recent history of Western societies themselves, as they transform in response to political, economic, security, and other factors;
hence the recent shift from the welfare state to more conservative economic and political policies in Western Europe and North America. A
preconceived view of human rights is even less tenable in non-Western
societies that seek to adapt Western political and economic models to
their own diverse contexts. To suggest the universalization of Western
models of state structures and powers does not mean that they are
replicated everywhere according to the same blueprint.

To summarize, the modern concept of human rights is the product
of a long history of struggle for social justice and resistance to oppression that is constantly adapting to changing conditions in order to better achieve its objectives. To the extent that the structures and processes
of social injustice and oppression are specific to each society, cultural
and contextual relativism—the claim that a society should live by its
own norms and values—exerts a pull. Conversely, as local particularities diminish under the force of globalization, the push for universal
human rights becomes more common. But since globalization reflects
the unequal power relations between developed and developing countries, the tension between the relative and universal will remain. To
keep this unavoidable tension from repudiating the concept of human
rights and frustrating its purpose in different societies, there must be a
deliberate effort to build an overlapping consensus around the normative content and implementation mechanisms of human rights.[7] That is,
the project of the universality of human rights is to be realized through
a congruence of societal responses to injustice and oppression, not by
transplanting a fully developed concept and its mechanisms of implementation from one society to another.

From a practical point of view, human rights norms are traditionally enacted in national constitutions and laws for domestic application

---

7. See John Rawl's "The Idea of an Overlapping Consensus," *Oxford Journal of Legal
Studies* 7, no. 1 (1987): 1–25. This idea is applied to the justification of universal human
rights in different cultures by several authors from different perspectives in An-Na'im
and Deng, *Human Rights in Africa,* and An-Na'im, *Cross-Cultural Perspective.*

by the judicial and executive organs of the state. Prior to the emergence of the modern human rights paradigm, the state was taken to have exclusive "territorial jurisdiction" in defining and implementing whatever level of protection of human rights it deemed fit. Since experience has shown that the state cannot be trusted to adequately protect the rights of all persons and groups within its territorial jurisdiction, the modern concept of human rights emerged as a means of ensuring certain minimum standards everywhere. Some of these minimum standards, like the prohibition of genocide, slavery, and torture, have evolved as customary international law binding on all states. But as a general rule, standards for human rights are articulated in international treaties that are binding only on states that have ratified them.[8] Paradoxically, however, the protection and implementation of both customary and treaty-based human rights is still completely dependent on the action of the state through its own legislative, judicial, and executive organs. Although the purpose of the modern concept of human rights is to restrict the exclusive power of the state, it is the same state that controls the means by which that purpose is to be achieved.

This paradox is the necessary consequence of the fundamental principle of state sovereignty on which the present international system is premised, as entrenched in the Charter of the United Nations and reiterated in numerous instruments.[9] Indeed, state sovereignty is the practical manifestation of the collective human right to self-determination. It is unlikely that states will relinquish their own autonomy by abandoning traditional notions of sovereignty or allow them to be undermined by other actors. More importantly for our purposes here, a frontal attack on the principle of sovereignty can also be counterpro-

---

8. For a review of the historical and conceptual development of international human rights law see Henry Steiner and Philip Alston, *International Human Rights in Context: Law, Politics, Morals* (Oxford: Clarendon Press, 1996), 117–65; and Francisco Forrest Martin et al., eds., *International Human Rights Law and Practice: Cases, Treaties, and Materials* (London: Klumer Law International, 1997), 1–4. On the sources of international human rights see Martin et al., 25–41.

9. Article 2(7) of the Charter of the United Nations, 1945; and Declaration on International Law Concerning Friendly Relations and Co-operation among States, GA Res. 2625, Annex UN GAOR, 25th Sess. (Supp. No. 28 at 122), UN Doc. A/8028; ELM 1292 (1970). In relation to African states see, for example, Young, *African Colonial State*, 27–30. See further, generally, Edmond J. Keller and Donald Rothchild, *Africa in the New International Order: Rethinking State Sovereignty and Regional Security* (Boulder, Colo.: Lynne Rienner, 1996).

ductive for the protection of human rights. Despite its problems, state sovereignty remains the essential expression of the fundamental right to self-determination, the practical vehicle of domestic policy, and the necessary medium of international relations. The sovereignty of the state is also a necessary safeguard against the control and manipulation of national economies by intergovernmental financial institutions (the World Bank and International Monetary Fund) or transnational corporations. A realistic and appropriate objective, therefore, is to diminish the negative consequences of the paradox of self-regulation by infusing the ethos of human rights into the fabric of the state itself and the global context in which it operates. The challenge is to address the structural, cultural, and other root causes of violations in order to implement human rights in a more systematic and comprehensive manner.

The paradox of self-regulation is further complicated in the case of most African countries by the nature and functioning of the postcolonial state, especially as the instrument of the protection and implementation of human rights.

> African states are direct successors of the European colonies that were alien entities to most of Africa. Their legitimacy derived not from internal African consent, but from international agreements—primarily among European states—beginning with the Berlin Conference of 1884–85. Their borders were usually defined not by African political facts or geography, but rather by international rules of continental partition and occupation established for that purpose. Their governments were organized according to European colonial theory and practice (tempered by expediency), and were staffed almost entirely by Europeans at decision-making levels. Their economies were managed with imperial and/or local colonial considerations primarily in mind. Their laws and policies reflected the interests and values of European imperial power, and these usually included strategic military uses, economic advantage, Christianization, European settlement, and so forth. Although the populations of the colonies were overwhelmingly African, the vast majority of the inhabitants had little or no constitutional standing in them.[10]

10. Robert H. Jackson and Carl G. Rosberg, "Sovereignty and Underdevelopment: Juridical Statehood in the African Crisis," *Journal of Modern African Studies* 24 (1986): 5–6.

When independence was eventually achieved, it was juridical statehood under international law more than empirical sovereignty on the ground. Since then, the preservation of juridical statehood and territorial integrity, rather than promotion of the ability and willingness of the state to live up to the practical requirements of sovereignty, has become the primary concern. As Chabal put it, the "post-colonial state in Africa was, with few exceptions, both overdeveloped and soft. It was overdeveloped because it was erected, artificially, on the foundations of the colonial state. It did not grow organically from within civil society. It was soft because, although in theory all-powerful, it scarcely had the administrative and political means of its dominance. Neither did it have an economic basis on which to rest political power."[11]

It is unrealistic to expect the postcolonial state to effectively protect human rights when it is the product of colonial rule that is by definition the negation of these rights. However one evaluates precolonial African political regimes from the point of view of human rights, it is clear that colonialism was incapable of creating and sustaining the institutions and processes necessary to protect rights. Therefore, independence usually signified the transfer of control over authoritarian power structures and processes of government from colonial masters to local elites.[12] Since the newly independent state usually lacked effective presence in most of its territory, ruling elites tended to focus on the government apparatus and patronage system. They also strove to retain the support of key traditional leaders, instead of seeking popular legitimacy and accountability to the people at large.[13] With their territorial integrity preserved primarily through membership of the United Nations and the Organization of African Unity, state security became the security of the regime in power, with no possibility of the transparency of the functioning of security forces, or of their political and legal accountability for their actions. Unable to govern effectively and humanely, postcolonial governments tended to use authoritarian methods to control political dissent through the same legal and institutional mechanisms initially set by

11. Patrick Chabal, "Introduction: Thinking about Politics in Africa," in *Political Domination in Africa: Reflections on the Limits of Power,* ed. Patrick Chabal (Cambridge: Cambridge University Press, 1986), 13.

12. See, for example, John A. A. Ayoade, "States without Citizens: An Emerging African Phenomenon," in *The Precarious Balance: State and Society in Africa,* ed. Donald Rothchild and Naomi Chazan (Boulder, Colo.: Westview Press, 1988), 104.

13. Ibid., 107–15.

colonial powers and maintained by several cycles of "native" governments since independence.[14]

Given these features of the postcolonial state, one can hardly
expect much viability or efficacy for the idea that government must be
in accordance with the rule of law that upholds the fundamental individual and collective rights of all citizens. Constitutional instruments
have also failed to hold governments legally or politically accountable
to their own citizens.[15] This general weakness of the principle of constitutionalism was compounded by the suspension or radical alteration of
first constitutions by military usurpers or single-party states within a
few years from independence. Irrespective of the explanation one
accepts, it is clear that local people were unwilling or unable to resist
the erosion of the rule of law and manipulation of state powers and
institutions by civilian and military governments alike.[16] Far from having a sense of ownership, expectation of protection and service, and a
general belief in their ability to influence its functioning, most African
societies regarded the postcolonial state with profound mistrust. They
tolerated its existence as an unavoidable evil and preferred the slightest
possible interaction with its institutions and processes.[17]

Nevertheless, there are indications of countertrends in popular
resistance and local activism within civil society supported by some
international actors and factors.[18] It is in this light that one can expect

---

14. On the crisis of the postcolonial state and the search for explanations see Young,
African Colonial State, 2–12. Young discusses this situation as "the integral state" (287–90),
which he defines as "a design of perfected hegemony, whereby the state seeks to achieve
unrestricted domination over civil society."

15. See H. W. Okoth-Ogendo, "Constitutions without Constitutionalism: Reflections on an African Political Paradox," and Issa G. Shivji, "State and Constitutionalism: A
New Democratic Perspective," both in *State and Constitutionalism: An African Debate on
Democracy*, ed. Issa G. Shivji (Harare, Zimbabwe: Southern African Political Economy
Series Trust, 1991), 3–25 and 27–54, respectively. Other chapters in this book examine
issues of nation building, military rule, single-party states, social movements, and related
matters in different parts of the continent.

16. See, for example, Michaele S. Pietrowski, "The One-Party State as a Threat to
Civil and Political Liberties in Kenya," in *Africa, Human Rights and the Global System: The
Political Economy of Human Rights in a Changing World*, ed. Eileen McCarthy-Arnolds,
David R. Penna, and Debra Joy Cruz Sobrepena (Westport, Conn.: Greenwood Press,
1994), 131–46.

17. Young, *African Colonial State*, 5.

18. Ibid., 218–43; Pita Ogaba Agbese, "The State versus Human Rights Advocates in
Africa: The Case of Nigeria," in McCarthy-Arnolds, Penna, and Sobrepena, *Africa Human
Rights*, 147–72. See generally, Claude E. Welch Jr., *Protection of Human Rights in Africa:
Roles and Strategies of Non-governmental Organizations* (Philadelphia: University of Penn-
sylvania Press, 1995).

better prospects for more effective protection and systematic implementation of human rights in Africa today. This expectation, however,
must be based on a realistic understanding of the situation as it is,
rather than how one would like it to be. Part of this realistic approach is
what might be called the "recolonization" of Africa.

Notwithstanding the mixed motives of both sides, human rights
were cited by African nationalist leaders in demanding independence,
as well as by European colonial powers in conceding to those demands.
Accordingly, the protection and implementation of human rights
became part of the raison d'être of the postcolonial state. Ironically,
however, human rights can also be associated with the mutual cooperation of European powers and African nationalist leaders in a new
recolonization of Africa that allowed colonial relations of power to continue.[19] By this I mean the increasing dependency of former African
colonies on their colonial powers. An example is the continued French
military presence in several western and central African countries to
"keep the peace" by maintaining dictatorial and corrupt regimes in
power.[20] More significant evidence of the diverse forms of dependency
is to be found in the daily economic activities, political processes, and
security arrangements, as well as the legal, administrative, and educational systems of most African states in their relations with former colonial powers. These dependencies continue to intensify under the growing globalization of the postcolonial world.

In current usage, the term *globalization* refers to, inter alia, transformation of the relations among states, institutions, groups, and individuals; the universalization of certain practices, identities, and structures;
and the global restructuring that has occurred in recent decades within
the framework of modern capitalist relations. Most recent definitions of
globalization emphasize

But this dimension of the politics of human rights should be understood in light of
the specific nature and context of civil society in Africa. On this see Patrick Chabal, *Power
in Africa: An Essay in Political Interpretation* (London: Macmillan, 1992), 82–97.

19. See Daniel C. Bach, "Reappraising Postcolonial Geopolitics: Europe, Africa, and
the End of the Cold War," and Shehu Othman, "Postscript: Legitimacy, Civil Society, and
the Return of Europe," both in *Legitimacy and the State in Twentieth-Century Africa: Essays
in Honour of A. H. Kirk-Greene*, ed. Terence Ranger and Olufemi Vaughan (London:
Macmillan, 1993), 247–57 and 258–62, respectively.

20. See, for example, Ibrahim A. Gambari, "The Role of Foreign Intervention in
African Reconstruction," in *Collapsed States: The Disintegration and Restoration of Legitimate
Authority*, ed. I. William Zartman (Boulder, Colo.: Lynne Rienner, 1995), 225–28.

an emerging system characterized by interdependence, flows and exchanges, the role of new technologies, the integration of markets, the shrinking of time and space, particularly, the intensification of world-wide social relations which link distinct localities in such a way that local happenings are shaped by events occurring miles away and vice-versa. . . . [But in such definitions] there is a resounding silence with regard to the importance of notions such as coercion, conflict, polarization, domination, inequality, exploitation and injustice. . . . [T]here is little or nothing about monopolies, disruptions and dislocations of the labor and other markets, the emergence of a global regulatory chaos and possible anomie and how these are being exploited for gains.[21]

Since globalization is the expression of existing power relations, it has become the means by which developed countries sustain their economic and political hegemony over developing countries. That is, as the instrument of whatever patterns of power exist between most African and Western states, which continue to be power relations of colonial dependency despite juridical sovereignty, globalization has become the vehicle of recolonization. Should those power relations be transformed to reflect partnership in development and more equitable distribution of wealth and power around the world, globalization will become the instrument of justice and liberation for all human societies.

For the purposes of this chapter, the real irony of the continuity of colonial power relations is that reliance on the legal protection of human rights has become a conservative force, minimizing risks of change in the status quo by the inadequacy of their slow, piecemeal, and state-centered approach. Could it be argued that by promising relief or remedy on a case-by-case basis, legal protection diverts efforts and resources from more systematic approaches to implementation of human rights—indeed seeks to delegitimize those approaches as too radical or counterproductive? The paradox of state self-regulation in the realization of human rights is more striking in the context of single-party states, military rule, and other problems of constitutionalism in Africa noted earlier. Instead of realizing its liberating potential during the struggle for independence, the modern human rights paradigm actually enables

---

21. Tade Akin Aina, "Globalization and Social Policy in Africa: Issues and Research Directions," CODESRIA Working Paper Series 6/96, 1997, Dakar, Senegal, 11.

leaders to maintain political power and economic privilege without delivering on their promises to protect these rights. This state of affairs could not have been sustained without the collaboration of the former colonial powers, in exchange for the acquiescence of those African leaders in the recolonization of their countries through globalization. Claims of legal protection of human rights are legitimizing this state of affairs by making promises of remedies it is incapable of keeping.

Moreover, since conditions and requirements for effective legal protection of human rights are lacking in most African postcolonial states, the human rights paradigm is unlikely to have the same liberating power it has in developed Western countries.[22] Although the problem is the lack of conditions and requirements, it can be argued that the modem conception of human rights itself is an instrument of social injustice and repression. In contrast to their earlier association with decolonization, human rights have become associated with recolonization; emphasis on the legal protection of these rights is unable to check the massive violations that occur in the daily life of the vast majority of persons and groups who are subject to the jurisdiction of the postcolonial state in Africa.

Under these circumstances, people become disillusioned with the concept of human rights, but what they should reject is the application of that concept in African countries in the same way it is applied in Western developed countries. If not challenged, such disillusionment can breed relativist claims that African societies are bound only by their own cultural and religious values and norms, as opposed to international standards of human rights. This is unacceptable because it repudiates the principle that human rights are due to every human being, without distinction on grounds of race, gender, religion, or national origin.

I suggest that what should be rejected is the universalization of specific assumptions and institutional arrangements for the legal protection of human rights, with little possibility for innovation and local adaptation. If human rights are to be truly universal, their normative content as well as mechanisms of implementation must reflect a consensus that emerges from the actual experiences of all human societies, while at the same time accepting the diversity and specificity of those experiences. That is, the universality of human rights should be

---

22. See Julius Ihonvbere, *The Political Economy of Crisis and Underdevelopment in Africa: Selected Works of Claude Ake,* ed. Julius Ihonvbere (Lagos, Nigeria: JAD Publishers, 1989), 86–90.

premised upon cultural and contextual particularities, rather than pretending that these specifics are nonexistent or unimportant.

The preceding argument emphasizes the need for alternative approaches to the implementation of human rights in Africa; it does not suggest the total rejection of the legal protection of human rights as such. On the contrary, the best alternative approaches include the enhancement of legal protection, as explained in the next section. However, legal protection must not only be sought through the actual means available to African societies and in the manner appropriate to their own context, but must also be supplemented by other strategies of implementation, as suggested in this chapter.

II.   Scope and Efficacy of the Legal Protection of Human Rights in Africa

Efforts to enhance legal protection of human rights in Africa should begin with a clear understanding of the inadequacy of the present concept and mechanisms of legal protection. In this light I propose a reconceptualization of legal protection as *part of wider strategies of implementation,* rather than as the primary means of realizing respect for human rights. A critique of the scope and quality of legal protection of rights may also indicate the nature and direction of broader strategies of implementation of human rights that should be adopted. For the purposes of this critique, I will take the Universal Declaration of Human Rights of 1948 as a framework for evaluating performance. Although not a binding treaty, the Universal Declaration is the founding instrument of the modern human rights paradigm, which has been adopted by all African states and incorporated into national constitutions of the majority of African states as well as into the African Charter on Human and Peoples Rights of 1981 as the authoritative regional human rights treaty.

By its own terms, the mandate of the Universal Declaration is simply the obligation to provide effective redress for every violation of human dignity and the rights of any person or group. For example, Article 25 provides that everyone has a "right to a standard of living adequate for the health and well-being of himself and his family, including food, clothing, housing and medical care and necessary social services." The clear meaning of this provision is that these economic and social rights are as much human rights as are life, liberty, and security of person (Article 3), protection against torture and cruel, inhuman, or degrading treatment or punishment (Article 5), equality before the law without discrimination (Article 7), and freedom of opinion and expression (Article 19). Yet there is little objection to the denial of basic needs of food, shelter, and medical care to the majority of human beings in Africa today.

The clear intent of the Universal Declaration is that violation of any of the rights and freedoms it provides for must be equally condemned and redressed, regardless of their source or cause. There is nothing in its language that limits human rights to the model of narrow justiciability that requires the identification of an individual victim, violator, and judicial remedy, as explained below. On the contrary, Article 28 provides that "everyone is entitled to a social and international order in which the rights and freedoms set forth in this Declaration can be fully realized." That is, human beings around the world whose right to an adequate standard of living is violated are entitled to whatever adjustments in the social and international order are necessary for the realization of their right to a standard of living adequate for the health of themselves and their families, including food, clothing, housing, medical care, and necessary social services. Such is the liberating promise of the Universal Declaration of Human Rights, as adopted by the General Assembly of the United Nations without dissent, and repeatedly endorsed in subsequent international and regional human rights treaties and national constitutions throughout the world.

Yet—and notwithstanding procedural differences among legal systems—narrowly conceived legal protection comes down to justiciability, which signifies the ability of a court of law to identify an individual victim, a violator, and to prescribe a remedy for the violation. According to this paradigm, when a person or group of persons believes that one of their individual human rights has been violated by a state policy or administrative action or the behavior of a state official, the aggrieved party or parties can sue for redress (or prosecute if criminal charges are warranted, as in a torture case) before a court of law. If the issue is not settled out of court, a trial may follow whereby the court will determine whether a violation has occurred and direct the implementation of appropriate remedy. For example, if a woman proves that she is being discriminated against on grounds of sex by legislation, state policy, or administrative action, or the behavior of a state official, a court will direct that the statute be repealed or order state officials to refrain from implementing the offending policy or administrative measure. In the case of an accused person who can show that he was convicted on the basis of a confession obtained under torture, the court will quash his conviction and order payment of compensation or punishment of the offending police officers when appropriate.

It is clear from these and similar examples that this conception of legal protection presupposes that the violation of rights is the exception rather than the rule, because the slow and expensive process of judicial vindication of rights cannot on a case-by-case basis cope with massive or systematic violations. Justiciability also assumes that potential victims have access to and can afford to pay for legal services, that the judiciary is independent and effective, that government officials will comply with court orders, and so forth. This model is not only limited, exclusive, expensive, and inaccessible to most Africans whose human rights are routinely violated by the state and nonstate actors, it is also incapable of redressing the type and scope of violations most frequently suffered. This is indeed a far cry from the "whatever it takes" approach of Article 28 of the Universal Declaration. This discrepancy, if unredressed, threatens the principle of the universality of human rights and defeats their essential purpose. How did this discrepancy between the expressed mandate of the Universal Declaration, on the one hand, and the legal protection of human rights, on the other, come about? The reasons for this discrepancy partly precede the adoption of the Universal Declaration, but most arise from the political and economic context in which human rights are supposed to be implemented in African countries today.

According to the modern human rights paradigm, every person is entitled to certain claims as of right against the state. In its traditional constitutional origins, the paradigm requires the state to refrain from infringing on the civil liberties of citizens, such as freedoms of expression and association, protection against torture and inhuman or degrading treatment or punishment, and so forth. Though the primary responsibility of the state under this conception is said to be "negative" in the sense of refraining from violating these rights through the actions or omissions of its own officials, the implementation of human rights actually entails expenditure and affirmative action. For example, respect for the right to the protection of the due process of the law requires allocation of resources and implementation of educational and administrative policies to maintain a credible and constitutionally valid administration of justice. Prohibition of discrimination and requirement of equal protection of the law have been interpreted to mandate an active role for the state in affirmative action programs. In this light, the "negative" view of human rights as merely requiring the state to refrain from violating rights, without a "positive" obligation to act in an affirmative sense, is no longer true of even the domestic constitutional theory and practice of liberal Western societies.

At the international level, as noted earlier, the concept of human rights has included, from the beginning of the United Nations era, affirmative or positive economic, social, and cultural rights, as well as traditional negative civil and political rights. However, despite frequent affirmation of the indivisibility and interdependence of these two sets of rights, it is clear that economic, social, and cultural rights were not supposed to enjoy equal status and effective implementation with civil and political rights.[23] Although the primary reasons for this dichotomy and hierarchy of rights were ideological and cultural, especially in the context of the Cold War, the declared rationale was said to be a matter of justiciability, ability to monitor and evaluate performance, and possibility of specific remedy. According to this logic, claims of civil and political rights are specific and concrete enough to be litigated in a court of law that can determine whether a violation has been committed, by whom, and what should be the remedy.

The nonjusticiability and nondeterminacy of economic, social, and cultural rights became a self-fulfilling prophecy since no effort was made to develop the appropriate definition and procedural methods for judicial enforcement of these rights, as was done for civil and political rights, in an incremental process. That is, there was a time when civil and political rights too were nonjusticiable and nondeterminant, but they were made justiciable and sufficiently determinant through imaginative development of judicial mechanisms and remedies. The same can happen to economic, social, and cultural rights. Now that some imaginative effort is being applied to these rights, positive results

---

23. Statement to the World Conference on Human Rights on behalf of the UN Committee on Economic, Social, and Cultural Rights, UN Doc. E/I 993/22, Annex III, pars. 2 and 5. The view that economic, social, and cultural rights are of lower status is reflected in the language of treaties and mechanisms for their implementation.

are emerging.[24] In any case, since these rights are as important as civil and political rights, ways must be found for their implementation, whether through appropriate adaptation of justiciability to the nature of these rights, or by nonjudicial means. But this approach presupposes a capacity for legal protection of human rights, which is hardly adequate even for civil and political rights in most African countries. Although there is great need for the better protection of civil and political rights, the need for implementation of economic, social, and cultural rights is desperate. The obvious conclusion is that the improbability of legal enforcement for economic, social, and cultural rights in Africa necessitates the development of alternative strategies of implementation.

The situation is even worse for collective rights, which are nominally acknowledged as an exception to the norm of individual rights. Common Article 1 of International Covenant on Civil and Political Rights and the International Covenant on Economic, Social and Cultural Rights, both of 1966, provides for the collective right to self-determination, yet no provision is made for the implementation of this right, through legal protection or otherwise. Once again, inefficacy is a self-fulfilling prophecy, and the collective right to self-determination remains the least developed among all human rights standards. Other collective rights, such as the right to development or protection of cultural identity, have also been subject to neglect and hostility. With minimal prospects for legal protection for such collective rights, alternative strategies for the implementation in the sense suggested in this chapter may be the only viable way to proceed.

Even for civil and political rights, the scope and quality of legal protection in most African societies is far from that envisaged by the modern paradigm of human rights. As stated earlier, that conception of

---

24. Examples of this creative approach to the implementation of economic, social, and cultural rights can be found under the constitutions of India (Articles 39–46) and South Africa (Articles 23–29). On the Indian experience see Upendra Baxi, "Judicial Discourse: The Dialectics of the Face and the Mask," *Journal of the Indian Law Institute* 35 (1993): 1.

Nongovernmental organizations such as Shelter Rights Initiative (Bank Chambers, Anambra House, 3d Floor, 27/29, Martins Street, Lagos, Tel/Fax 266 2947), are striving to realize these rights through a variety of strategies. See generally, Asbjorn Eide, Catarina Krause, and Allan Rosas, *Economic, Social, and Cultural Rights: A Textbook* (Dordrecht, Netherlands: Martinus Nijhoff, 1994).

legal protection presupposes a degree of political stability, economic resources, institutional capacity, and the willingness and ability of the public at large to resort to the courts for the enforcement of their rights. Legal protection also assumes the prevalence of a certain conception of the rule of law, independence of the judiciary, and executive compliance with judicial determinations. Few of these conditions can be sustained in postcolonial Africa.

Recent studies of the legal protection of human rights in some fifteen African countries (representing a cross-section of cultures, colonial and postcolonial experiences, and legal systems) identified the following common problems.[25]

1.   Despite differences between the two systems, common law and continental civil law, followed in almost all African countries today, regimes suffer from similar problems of poor legitimacy and accessibility, as well as lack of human material resources.[26] Neither common law nor civil law, both of which are foreign colonial legal systems, has gained public confidence as a means of protection.

2.   Most current African constitutions provide for the protection of civil and political rights, including broad nondiscrimination and equal protection clauses. Some constitutions, such as those of Ghana, Namibia, and Uganda, include economic, social, and cultural rights as "Directive Principles of State Policy." There is also a good level of ratification of international treaties on human rights. But at this normative level, effective implementation is hampered by such factors as the lack

---

25. See note 1 for the list of the countries covered. Not every study mentioned all the points made, but each point was supported by the all the studies that addressed it. These studies were conducted under the auspices of the project on the Legal Protection of Human Rights under Constitutions of Africa, co-organized by Interights (London) and Afronet (Lusaka, Zambia).

My remarks here also draw on the following documents prepared for this project: Cidi Anselm Odinkalu, "The Legal Protection of Human Rights under the Constitutions of Africa," Report of the Planning Meeting in Lusaka, Zambia, July 28–30, 1995; Chidi Anselm Odinkalu, "A Preliminary Report on Information and Training Resources for the Legal Protection of Human Rights," and the draft report of the proceedings of an international conference of some eighty African human rights lawyers and activists from thirty countries who convened in Dakar, Senegal, December 11–13, 1997.

All of these documents are on file at the offices of Interights in London; I am currently editing them for publication as a report of the project as a whole. A book containing the best country studies is also being edited for publication.

26. See, for example, Claude Ake, *Democratization of Disempowerment in Africa* (Lagos, Nigeria: Malthouse Press, 1994), 11–13.

of the incorporation of treaty obligations into domestic legislation, where it is required in common law jurisdiction; frequent and prolonged states of emergency; and claw back clauses permitting restriction of constitutional provisions by ordinary legislation.

3.   At a practical level, the protection of human rights is seriously impeded by its reliance on judicial enforcement that is weak for civil and political rights and inappropriate for economic, social, and cultural rights. Because of their conceptual complexity and procedural formality, both common and civil law are incomprehensible and financially inaccessible for the vast majority of African peoples. Moreover, state courts and law enforcement mechanisms are incapable of addressing massive violations of human rights that occur under customary and religious laws and practices at the local, rural level.

4.   These difficulties are compounded by general structural and contextual factors, such as political instability, economic underdevelopment, and lack of independence for, and poor training of, the judiciary, as well as poor quality and unavailability of legal services. These features, in turn, lead to inadequacy of courtroom facilities, lack of essential material resources, and rampant corruption. In Nigeria, for example, litigants have to provide the stationery (writing materials and file folders) required for their cases and are routinely subjected to extortion by magistrates and court personnel. Since the vast majority of the two hundred legal practitioners in the whole of Mozambique are concentrated in the capital, Maputo, the role of legal council in district courts is left to ad hoc "public defenders" who have no legal training.

Given these realities, to wait for all the prerequisite conditions of legal protection in the narrow sense, knowing that they are unlikely to materialize or work effectively, is to condemn human rights in Africa to empty political rhetoric and permanent marginality. Despite its limitations as the primary mechanism for the implementation of human rights, legal protection should be maintained and improved to achieve more protection with less capacity and fewer resources in the African context. But the sort of legal protection mandated by the "whatever it takes" approach of Article 28 of the Universal Declaration must be broader and more inclusive, affordable, and accessible. That approach also requires the sort of legal protection that is capable of redressing the type and scope of violations most frequently suffered.

The methods of such legal protection should include mediation, arbitration, and other customary mechanisms to resolve disputes that are more appropriate to social and economic conditions in Africa, as well as justiciability in the narrow sense. But the whole rationale and process of such customary mechanisms is hardly consistent with the notion of legal protection of rights in the formal, legalistic Western sense underlying the present paradigm. This does not mean that the two approaches cannot work together, but flexibility and imagination regarding who is entitled to what against whom under the human right in question are required. In fact, the application of such customary mechanisms will be so different from present notions of legal protection as to require a radical shift in the conception and implementation of human rights. Such a shift is also necessary if the structural approach to addressing root causes of violations, as suggested in this chapter, is to be taken seriously. The problem is that such shifts will probably be resisted by human rights activists themselves who have developed a vested interest in preserving the status quo and their role in it. But an appreciation of the need for alternative strategies is perhaps a necessary step in the right direction.

III. Addressing Root Causes

It is better to address root causes of human rights violations than to pursue legal remedies on a case-by-case basis, especially for most African societies, because it is more economical, comprehensive, sustainable, and humane. Coerced enforcement requires extensive human and material resources and is an approximation of redress that can never erase the pain and suffering of the violation or restore the victims to their prior situation. Moreover, any enforcement regime must assume a high level of compliance in order to deal effectively with exceptional violations. These and similar reasons in support of addressing root causes apply when legal protection is working well in developed societies but apply even more strongly where legal protection is weak and ineffective, as in postcolonial Africa.

However, addressing the root causes of human rights violations is an extremely complex and protracted task, for obvious reasons. As indicated earlier, many factors are at work, such as the level and quality of political commitment to the implementation of specific norms, availability of economic resources for their realization, and the ability to utilize the necessary administrative, educational, and legal reform. As these and other factors interact, it is difficult to isolate any one of them as a root cause of human rights violations. Moreover, it is simplistic and misleading to address any one of them in isolation from other factors and processes. In short, most of what can be described as root causes of human rights violations actually raise fundamental philosophical and ideological questions about the nature of the "good society" and how it can be realized in particular contexts. These factors, their interaction and consequences, are the subject matter of politics and social transformation everywhere.

For example, the lack of political commitment to the human rights of women is partly due to cultural resistance to the principle of equality and nondiscrimination on grounds of sex that is their foundation.[27] Political opposition to the human rights of women can also be promoted by men whose economic and social privileges are threatened. Equality for women challenges male dominance within the family and other social and political institutions, forces men to compete with women for jobs, compels employers to pay women equal wages and benefits, and requires the state to combat discrimination in education, provision of social services, access to employment, and so forth. Such political opposition will be reflected in resistance to the allocation of economic resources, to educational and administrative policies, and to law reforms necessary for the implementation of the human rights of women. Political or cultural opposition can also be reflected in administrative misconceptions, delay, and obstruction in the daily execution of formally approved policies.[28]

Another difficulty in addressing root causes of human rights violations is the allocation of limited human and economic resources among competing public policy objectives. Even if one assumes the political commitment and cultural support for the implementation of

27. Cf. Arati Rao, "The Politics of Gender and Culture in International Human Rights Discourse," and Ann E. Mayer, "Cultural Particularism as a Bar to Women's Rights: Reflections on the Middle East," both in *Women's Rights, Human Rights: International Feminist Perspectives*, ed. Julie Peters and Andrea Wolper (New York: Routledge, 1995), 167–75 and 176–88, respectively.

28. On the problems and possibilities of the implementation of the human rights of women in Africa, see Abdullahi A. An-Na'im, "State Responsibility under International Human Rights Law to Change Religious and Customary Laws," Chaloka Beyani, "Toward a More Effective Guarantee of Women's Rights in the African Human Rights System," Adetoun O. Ilumoka, "African Women's Economic, Social, and Cultural Rights," and Florence Butegwa, "Using the African Charter on Human and Peoples' Rights to Secure Women's Access to Land in Africa," all in *Human Rights of Women: National and International Perspectives*, ed. Rebecca J. Cook (Philadelphia: University of Pennsylvania Press, 1994), 167–88, 285–306, 307–25, and 495–514, respectively.

the human rights of women, priorities have to be set between this and other objectives of public policy, such as investment in economic development or meeting security needs of the country. These choices are in turn affected by philosophical and ideological considerations, for example, the proper role of the state in the provision of education, health care, and other economic and social rights.

The consequences of these domestic dynamics are linked to structural factors in global and bilateral relations of economic and political power. Those external factors not only limit the availability of economic resources to most African states, but also restrict their freedom to implement national policies permitted by existing resources. Structural factors in production and trade relations between developed and African countries condemn the latter to the role of producers of raw materials and consumers of goods manufactured elsewhere. In this unequal relationship, most African countries must accept whatever prices developed countries are willing to pay for raw materials, while paying high prices for the import of manufactured goods because of the added value of these goods due to investment and services provided by developed countries.

Moreover, because of their economic and technological superiority, developed countries prescribe for most African countries the scope and direction of their own economic development and social policy through bilateral and multilateral "aid and development assistance" programs. Burdened with interest on loans, with little prospect of paying the capital, most African countries are forced to implement "structural adjustment programs" that require them to reduce government spending. Given the nature of the postcolonial state in Africa and prevalence of certain cultural norms and practices, the implementation of human rights is the first victim of these restrictions.

The analysis of this chapter leads me to pose the issue in terms of a fundamental global as well as local responsibility for the implementation of human rights. Recalling the "all it takes" mandate of the Universal Declaration of Human Rights, it is simply unacceptable to blame African victims for the complicity of their ruling elites with powerful economic and political forces in the so-called international community. Far from discharging this mandate, legal protection in the narrow sense of the term can in fact be part of the problem in creating the false hope of relief and wasting the energy and resources of the few local and international advocates of human rights. Given the requisite political commitment by all relevant actors, the difficulties of addressing root causes can be resolved, and legal protection can play its appropriate role in the implementation of human rights. Here are some elements of an alternative strategy for the effective implementation of human rights in Africa.

First, there should be an honest and candid appreciation of the limitations of the present paradigm, especially its reliance on legal protection in isolation from structural, cultural, and other root causes of violations. Narrowly conceived legal protection cannot cope with the scale of human rights violations.

Second, a serious commitment to the implementation of human rights as envisaged by the Universal Declaration requires drastic structural changes in international economic and political relations. The fate of the United Nations initiative to establish a New International Economic Order,[29] as continued by the Group of 77, shows that no significant adjustments in global economic and political relations can be achieved without the consent of, and leadership by, developed countries. In view of the nature of the postcolonial state in Africa, international initiatives must be weighed carefully, for it cannot be assumed which initiatives would improve human rights.

Third, commitment to the implementation of human rights requires addressing delicate and complex issues of sovereignty and the paradox of self-regulation. Though national governments cannot be trusted to regulate their own behavior, unilateral action or intervention by major powers is also dangerous and usually counterproductive. The best

---

29. This effort of developing countries to redress their economic and political relations with developed countries gathered some momentum in the 1960s and 1970s, as reflected in such United Nations instruments as Resolutions 1803 of 1962 and 3171 of 1973, on Permanent Sovereignty over Natural Resources, Resolution 3201 of 1974, Declaration on the Establishment of a New International Economic Order, Resolution 3201 of 1974; and Resolution 3281 of 1974, the Charter of Economic Rights and Duties of States.

This initiative has been continued, in some respects, by what is known as the Group of 77 (now more than 120) African, Asian, and Latin American countries. This group has found institutional staff support in the United Nations' Conference on Trade and Development (UNCTAD) which has become, in many ways, a counter-balance to the Organization for Economic Cooperation and Development (OECD), the Paris-based organization that includes most of the industrialized countries. In 1993, the Group of 77 revised its 1981 Caracas Action Program for coordinating efforts in eight key areas: energy, finance, food and agriculture, industrialization, raw materials, technical cooperation, trade, and technology. Since the early 1990s, however, the group has found it difficult to maintain unity on its objectives, as more developing countries began to opt for bilateral negotiations with industrialized countries.

approach, therefore, may be more effective implementation through multilateral action, whether through the United Nations and its specialized agencies, or some other international or regional mechanism.

Fourth, insofar as legal protection plays a role in human rights, its methods must be adapted to the actual conditions in different societies. In particular, the traditional notion of justiciability should be examined critically to improve its application where it is appropriate, and it should be replaced with other strategies and mechanisms where it is inappropriate or ineffective.

Fifth, in these and other strategies for addressing the root causes of violations of human rights, whatever good or bad happens in the world happens through the moral choices each of us makes. All violations are committed by human beings acting or failing to act, whether they are the direct perpetrators of the wrong or persons who let it happen. As I write, human rights are being violated all over the world. The ultimate question is simply this: what am I doing to prevent this or the next violation?

Whatever view one may take of the root causes of human rights violations in Africa, the practical question is who is going to address them, and how? In view of the problematic nature and role of the postcolonial state, one might look to nongovernmental organizations for initiative and leadership, though their efforts must be implemented through state organs and agencies. But besides the lack of resources and restrictive political conditions facing nongovernmental organizations, there is the problem of what I call "human rights dependency." Human rights initiatives in most African countries originate from foreign sources, not from within, and are addressed to foreign governments, not African governments. In contrast to developed countries, where human rights are protected by local organizations acting through their own political and legal institutions against offending officials, policies, or legislation, such international organizations as Amnesty International and Human Rights Watch play this role in most African countries. These international organizations monitor human rights to report them to their constituencies in developed countries, who are expected to influence their governments to pressure African governments into respecting the human rights of their populations.

Although the number of local human rights organizations in African countries is growing, this dependency model continues, for several reasons. First, local organizations tend to adopt the operational style of international organizations, monitoring and reporting violations through international media in order to generate pressure on their own governments from foreign rather than local sources. Second, since local organizations tend to find funding from foreign agencies and foundations, they do not feel the need to build local constituencies for material and political support. But the consequence of this state of affairs is that local organizations remain isolated from their communities, perpetuating human rights dependency. Third, African governments take advantage of the situation by oppressing local activists without fear of political consequences at home, while challenging the credibility of international organizations as agents of foreign cultural imperialism.

The preceding remarks are not intended to suggest that monitoring by international human rights organizations should stop, or that local African organizations should change their operational methods. In view of the economic, political, security, and other dependencies of most African states on former colonial powers and other developed countries, this dependency is both unavoidable and useful, at least in the short term. Instead, I am calling for change in the attitudes and operational style of international and local nongovernmental organizations in order to gradually diminish this dependency by promoting internal initiatives and processes. In my view, local organizations are more likely to understand, and to have greater credibility in addressing, cultural, economic, or political root causes of human rights violations. Local organizations certainly need material and technical support of international organizations, especially protection of their right and ability to operate effectively in their own countries, but this should be in the nature of partnership, not dependency. This dual approach—more effective legal protection and addressing root causes—depends on sufficient commitment among local and international constituencies to do "whatever it takes" for the implementation of human rights.

Having argued that most African societies can do more for human rights with less reliance on legal protection—what sounds like heresy from a lawyer—I conclude with what sounds like a heresy from a human rights advocate: Humanity has existed in the past without the modern human rights paradigm and will survive its demise. Indeed, the struggle for social justice and resistance to oppression will continue through whatever means are available to people everywhere in the world. The human rights movement will stand or fall by its own record of achievement in each society's struggle for human dignity and social justice. To say that the human rights movement will be condemned to permanent marginality if it fails to deliver on its promises is simply to state the obvious.

Contributors

Abdullahi A. An-Na'im is Professor of Law at Emory University.

Homi K. Bhabha is Charles Tripp Professor in the Humanities at the University of Chicago.

Jane F. Collier is Professor of Anthropology at Stanford University.

Thomas R. Kearns is the William H. Hastie Professor of Philosophy and Professor of Law, Jurisprudence, and Social Thought at Amherst College.

Austin Sarat is the William Nelson Cromwell Professor of Jurisprudence and Political Science and Professor of Law, Jurisprudence, and Social Thought at Amherst College, past-President of the Law and Society Association, and current President of the Association for the Study of Law, Culture, and the Humanities.

Iris Marion Young is Professor of Political Science at the University of Chicago.

Index